MW01277798

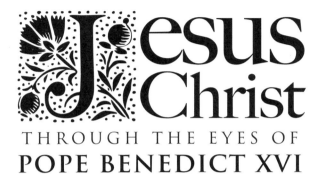

esus Christ

THROUGH THE EYES OF
POPE BENEDICT XVI

Edited by Giuliano Vigini

Libreria Editrice Vaticana
United States Conference of Catholic Bishops
Washington, DC

CONTENTS

PREFACE

Faith and Life in Christ in the Thought of Benedict XVI

At the center of the Magisterium of the Church is the experience, the proclamation, and the testimony of the mystery of salvation revealed by God in Christ, Lord and Savior of all. In committing itself to performing this ministry, consubstantial with its life and mission, the Church hands down with integrity and coherence the patrimony of faith that it has received, but at the same time receives the particular imprint—of thought, vision, and style—that confers on it little by little its supreme guidance in transmitting it to the men and women of its time. From one pope to the next, therefore, although in the same tension toward the common goal,[1] there are different pastoral decisions and directions in the manner of helping people to "think" the faith and to live it, and this "diversity" represents a richness for the Church that, through the pope and the pastors united with him in episcopal collegiality, communicates in a way always new the perennial truths.

Benedict XVI is pursuing the goal—in stages, but according to an orderly plan—of presenting the foundations of the faith in an organic manner, in order to offer as

---

1 This "tension" is—to use the words of Paul VI—the "supreme awareness" of needing to call everyone, "to reveal to them the truth, to make them children of God and brethren of one another": cf. Paul VI, *Pensiero alla morte*, Vatican City, Libreria Editrice Vaticana (LEV) (1978), p.n.n.

clear and unified a vision of it as possible. He is doing this as theologian and as pastor, the one firmly grafted into the other, through preaching dense with content, always substantiated by the Bible and by the Fathers of the Church—beginning with his beloved Augustine[2]—but always attentive also to expressing himself in language comprehensible to all. In this way emerge the profundity of doctrine, the wisdom of the Gospel, and the paternal benevolence[3] with which Benedict XVI engages his whole self in making known and savored the beauty of the Christian faith, certain that the truth of God incarnate of Jesus Christ also encloses the fullness of the truth of man.

The first challenge consists in "making God visible in the human face of Christ."[4] To those who, in the search for their identity and in the assertion of their freedom, have distanced themselves from God, becoming lost and even becoming "strangers to themselves,"[5] the pope addresses the heartbroken appeal to seek God,[6] and to the pastors the

---

2 See, in this same series, Benedict XVI, *Sant'Agostino spiegato dal Papa*, edited by Giuliano Vigini, Vatican City, LEV (2010).

3 Even "ordinary people perceive the truth and grasp the meaning of a faith and a human wisdom rich with paternity": inverview with Cardinal Tarcisio Bertone, "Il progetto di Chiesa e di societa' di Benedetto XVI," in *L'Osservatore Romano* (August 28, 2009), 8.

4 Address to the bishops of Ontario on their "ad limina" visit, in *Insegnamenti di Benedetto XVI*, 2/2006, Vatican City, LEV (2007), 2006.

5 Ibid., p. 207.

6 On this topic, see also the beautiful *Lettera ai cercatori di Dio*, prepared by the Episcopal Commission for the Doctrine, Proclamation, and Catechesis of the Faith, of the Italian Episcopal Conference (Cinsello Balsamo: Edizioni San Paolo, 2009).

encouragement to intensify their efforts to help all to find him. But those who set out on this path need "the evangelical capacity to be children at heart,"[7] which means having the authentic humility to leave behind one's own certainties, to recognize one's limitations, to surmount mental prejudices and psychological barriers, and thus to open the heart to God who made himself small precisely in order to draw near to us. In this frame of mind, one also receives the light to understand—as Benedict XVI emphatically reiterates in the most varied circumstances, following in the footsteps of John Paul II—that there is no real conflict between faith and reason, science and revelation, obedience and freedom, adherence to the faith and responsibility: a conflict that is often perceived as beyond remedy by contemporary culture.

With no less vigor, the appeals of the pope are addressed to believers, that they persevere in faith, allowing themselves to be guided and sustained by the wisdom of the Gospel, renewing their commitment[8] to letting themselves be shaped by the love of God and by generosity in responding to this gift of love, bearing witness to it in life. Those who strive to perfect themselves and to progress in God do not settle, do not stop, do not grow tired of continuing to search. The Christian is "one who seeks and one who finds,"[9] in the sense that—as Augustine notes (*Ennarationes*

---

7 Homily at the Mass of Epiphany (January 6, 2010): "L'umiltà e il coraggio di credere in un Bambino," in *L'Osservatore Romano* (January 7-8, 2010), 8.

8 *Deus Caritas Est*, Vatican City, LEV (2006), p. 7.

9 *Insegnamenti* . . . I, 1/2005, cit., p. 502.

in Psalmos 104, 3)—"to the extent to which love grows, the search grows for the one who has been found" (*Amore crescente, inquisitio crescat inventi*).[10] Because the search for God does not conclude with the discovery, but departs again and intensifies in proportion to love. It is no coincidence that Benedict XVI, in his first encyclical, has placed love at the center of the Christian faith, as "the Christian image of God and the resulting image of mankind and its destiny."[11] "God is love" (1 Jn 4:8, 16), and this love is not an abstraction, because in Jesus Christ, who came to live among us, the love of God has taken a face, has been manifested, has acted. And it continues to act, so that there may continue to grow in the Church and in society a community that grows by love and bears the life that is born from love. The love of God, in fact, is not fully realized if it does not involve the intimate sphere of man and is not put into practice in all of the forms in which Jesus instructed him. The reflection of Benedict XVI thus branches out in many directions. In the conjunction of the "great commandment" (Mt 22:36, 38) of the love of God and the "new commandment" (Jn 13:34; 1 Jn 2:7, 8; 2 Jn 5) of love of neighbor, he in fact finds himself constantly establishing connections and interactions between the love of God and the truth, between love and justice, between love and unity, between love and peace: the essential components on which the order of love is founded and perfected. This is the heart of the wisdom of the Gospel and the true foundational

---

10 Ibid. Cf. Augustine, *The Trinity*, IX, 1.1.

11 *Deus Caritas Est*, cit., p. 5.

principle of a society in which the common good becomes the end that one approaches while exercising love. This, therefore, is love: true, purified from "self-love" and from the "love of the world," which, by virtue of the gift of the Spirit, becomes a visible sign of the love of Christ. Each one is called, imitating this perfect model of love, to build a community of love. The social encyclical of Benedict XVI, *Caritas in Veritate*, is intended precisely to illustrate, in the various fields, how this power of love can and must be placed at the service of the comprehensive development of each person and of all humanity. The faith that is made concrete and strengthened in the exercise of "caritas" generates the true and transforming encounter with the living God, Jesus Christ, in whom resides all Christian hope, which already here on earth is manifested as "proof" of that which is not yet seen (Heb 11:1).[12]

Benedict XVI's discussion of the faith thus always goes right to the heart of the matter, with both the principles of doctrine and the experience of faith, as exemplified by the selections from his Magisterium that are presented here from among the many that could be selected to expound his thought and the character that he wishes to impart to the Church's journey. If it can be said that, over the forty years that have passed from the *Introduction to Christianity*[13]

---

12 On this point, cf. the exegesis proposed in the encyclical *Spe Salvi*, Vatican City, LEV, 2007, pp. 17-23.

13 Published in German in 1968, the work was translated in Italy in 1968 by Queriniana of Brescia and has been reprinted many times, in the new translation by Gianni Francesconi and with a new introduction by the author (2000).

to the first part of *Jesus of Nazareth*[14] there has been no substantial change in the basic perspective of Benedict XVI in presenting the "God of Jesus Christ,"[15] his figure and his message, it is clear that today, from the chair of Peter, for Benedict XVI not only does the responsibility to transmit the faith of the Church take on a greater weight and a wider scope, but the primary preoccupation becomes that of identifying the most effective way "to proclaim to the whole world the living presence of Christ."[16] If before him, in fact, there are always the distant whom he must reach with his voice, the believers to be strengthened in the faith, the brethren of other faiths with whom a fecund dialogue must be patiently constructed, this has aggravated and expanded the problems posed in today's society by the dramatic fracture between Gospel and culture.

The pope is well aware of the arduous challenges that he must face. Philosophies and ideas, behaviors and life-styles are clashing today, not only with the teaching of Christian doctrine, but also with the ethical and social values of Christianity, which should instead represent the master approach toward authentic human development. This situation has been determined by various causes, but foremost among these seems to be that false conception of freedom that has generated a culture of unbridled will, of which individualism and relativism have become the pillars of support. A freedom, in fact, that is reflected only in

---

14 Italian edition edited by Ingrid Stampa and Elio Guerriero; translated by Chicca Galli and Roberta Zupper, Milan, Rizzoli (2007).

15 Title of a theological-spiritual work originally published in 1976 and translated by Dino Pezzetta for Queriniana (1978).

16 *Insegnamenti di Benedetto XVI* I, 1/2005, Vatican City, LEV (2006), p. 9.

itself, excluding God and losing any connection with truth and goodness, loses its identity and ends up separating even public ethics from its *humus* of reference that gives it meaning and fullness. The disappearance of the meaning of life, so intimately connected to the person and to his hope for the future; the explosion of violence and abuse; the loss of the concept of authority; the emptying of the very idea of the "common good" are some of the consequences that can be situated within this context, which has also fostered the progressive disintegration of ethical awareness and responsibility.

The de-Christianization of society continues to go hand in hand with its secularization: a phenomenon that insidiously manifests itself in various forms also in the life of the Church and in the personal experience of believers, both as a general phenomenon of assimilation of the "spirit of the times" and as a specific phenomenon of "deviation" on the theological or pastoral level. In order to place within a context of synthesis the reflections and preoccupations of Benedict XVI, it should suffice to recall the approval of certain mentalities and behaviors, marked above all by a widespread climate of subjectivity and materialism, which find less resistance in a faith that has become weaker, and at the same time in greater psychological and emotional fragility on the part of persons, including the clergy; the tolerance toward attitudes and language that are in themselves worthy of condemnation, but so widespread as to be considered fully assimilated, such that fighting against them would be a senseless battle lost before it is begun; the adaptation or "aggiornamento" to demands or even fashions of the moment that drive people away from the heart of the Christian proclamation and, subordinating it to purely human demands, deform and impoverish it; the excessive emphasis on things of today, with the result of restricting the Christian vision to a functional and contingent dimension, forgetting its ancient roots and its broad horizons.

There should be added, on the level of the specific, the always lurking threat of rationalizing and relativizing the truths of the faith, bringing the risk of deforming, impoverishing, and obscuring the very essence of the Christian mystery; the blurring of the concept of authority, Magisterium, and obedience, which leads to theories or attitudes contrary to the teaching or discipline of the Church; religious syncretism, parallel to the spread of new forms of spirituality, but above all to the loss or weakening of the awareness of the distinctive truth of Christianity; a certain "philanthropization" of pastoral practice, to the extent to which this tends to favor charitable and social demands over the proclamation of Jesus Christ dead and risen; the personalization of the faith in a utilitarian sense, with the consequent relativization of the teachings of the Magisterium and the loss of the sense of belonging to the Church; the decline of the sense of sin, which becomes an open road to subjectivism in the area of morality, especially with regard to the family and to sexuality; the disjunction and profound separation between one's beliefs and inconsistent positions taken in the field of political decisions on questions of fundamental anthropological, ethical, and social significance.

Under another aspect, one cannot forget the recurrent intellectual distortions relative to the heritage of Vatican Council II, or the confusion generated by a false or partial interpretation: what Benedict XVI calls "the hermeneutic of discontinuity and rupture," counterposed by a correct and complete interpretation of the texts, "the hermeneutic of reform,"[17] which little by little spawns new reflections to respond more adequately to exigencies old and new, but holding firm the fidelity and continuity of the principles, certain and immutable, of the "deposit of the faith." Nor can one remain silent on the tendency among many to separate "Gospel and institution," in the sense of understanding the Gospel as a purely spiritual reality and the institution as a superficial structure, while in fact they are two inseparable entities, because "the Gospel has a body, the Lord has a body in this time of ours. Consequently, issues that seem at first sight merely institutional are actually theological and central, because it is a matter of the realization and concretization of the Gospel in our time."[18]

In this effort to explain and explore, clarify and correct, one grasps Benedict XVI's complete commitment to spending himself for the Gospel, as the vicar of Christ who speaks and acts, "not to impose the faith, but to call for courage for the truth."[19]

---

17 See the address to cardinals, bishops, and prelates of the Roman curia (December 22, 2005): *Una giusta ermeneutica per leggere e recepire il Concilio come grande forza di rinnovamento della Chiesa*, in *Insegnamenti di Benedetto XVI* I, 1/2005, Vatican City, LEV (2006), p. 1024.

18 *Insegnamenti di Benedetto XVI* II, 2/2006, Vatican City, LEV (2007), p. 595.

19 From the address on "Papacy and university" that Benedict XVI was scheduled to deliver at the University of Rome "La Sapienza"; cf. *Insegnamenti di Benedetto XVI* IV, 1/2008, Vatican City, LEV (2009), pp. 78-86.

TEXTS OF THE
POPE'S CATECHESES

They Shall Look on Him Whom They Have Pierced

Dear Brothers and Sisters!

"They shall look on him whom they have pierced" (Jn 19:37). This is the biblical theme that this year guides our Lenten reflection. Lent is a favorable time to learn to stay with Mary and John, the beloved disciple, close to him who on the Cross, consummated for all mankind the sacrifice of his life (cf. Jn 19:25). With a more fervent participation let us direct our gaze, therefore, in this time of penance and prayer, at Christ Crucified who, dying on Calvary, revealed fully for us the love of God. In the Encyclical *Deus Caritas Est*, I dwelt upon this theme of love, highlighting its two fundamental forms: *agape* and *eros*.

God's Love: *Agape* and *Eros*

The term *agape*, which appears many times in the New Testament, indicates the self-giving love of one who looks exclusively for the good of the other. The word *eros*, on the other hand, denotes the love of one who desires to possess what he or she lacks and yearns for union with the beloved. The love with which God surrounds us is undoubtedly *agape*. Indeed, can man give to God some good that he does not already possess? All that the human creature is and has is divine gift. It is the creature, then, who is in need of God in everything. But God's love is also *eros*. In the Old Testament, the Creator of the universe manifests toward the people whom he has chosen as his own a predilection that transcends every human motivation. The prophet Hosea expresses this divine passion with daring images such as the love of a man for an adulterous woman (cf. 3:1-3). For his part, Ezekiel, speaking of God's relationship with the people of Israel, is not afraid to use strong and passionate language (cf. 16:1-22). These biblical texts indicate that *eros* is part of God's very Heart: the Almighty awaits the "yes" of his creatures as a young bridegroom that of his bride. Unfortunately, from its very origins, mankind, seduced by the lies of the Evil One, rejected God's love in the illusion of a self-sufficiency that is impossible (cf. Gn 3:1-7). Turning in on himself, Adam withdrew from that source of life who is God himself, and became the first of "those who through fear of death were subject to lifelong bondage" (Heb 2:15). God, however, did not give up. On the contrary, man's "no" was the decisive impulse that moved him to manifest his love in all of its redeeming strength.

The Cross Reveals the Fullness of God's Love

It is in the mystery of the Cross that the overwhelming power of the Heavenly Father's mercy is revealed in all

of its fullness. In order to win back the love of his creature, he accepted to pay a very high price: the Blood of his
Only Begotten Son. Death, which for the first Adam was
an extreme sign of loneliness and powerlessness, was thus
transformed in the supreme act of love and freedom of the
new Adam. One could very well assert, therefore, together
with St. Maximus the Confessor, that Christ "died, if one
could say so, divinely, because he died freely" (*Ambigua*,
91, 1056). On the Cross, God's *eros* for us is made manifest.
Eros is indeed, as Pseudo-Dionysius expresses it, that force
which "does not allow the lover to remain in himself but
moves him to become one with the beloved" (*De Divinis
Nominibus*, IV, 13: PG 3, 712). Is there more "mad *eros*"
(N. Cabasilas, *Vita in Cristo*, 648) than that which led the
Son of God to make himself one with us even to the point
of suffering as his own the consequences of our offenses?

"Him Whom They Have Pierced"

Dear brothers and sisters, let us look at Christ pierced on
the Cross! He is the unsurpassing revelation of God's love,
a love in which *eros* and *agape*, far from being opposed,
enlighten each other. On the Cross, it is God himself who
begs the love of his creature: He is thirsty for the love of
every one of us. The Apostle Thomas recognized Jesus as
"Lord and God" when he put his hand into the wound
of his side. Not surprisingly, many of the saints found in
the Heart of Jesus the deepest expression of this mystery
of love. One could rightly say that the revelation of God's
eros toward man is, in reality, the supreme expression of

his *agape*. In all truth, only the love that unites the free gift of oneself with the impassioned desire for reciprocity instills a joy which eases the heaviest of burdens. Jesus said, "When I am lifted up from the earth, I will draw all men to myself" (Jn 12:32). The response the Lord ardently desires of us is above all that we welcome his love and allow ourselves to be drawn to him. Accepting his love, however, is not enough. We need to respond to such love and devote ourselves to communicating it to others. Christ "draws me to himself" in order to unite himself to me, so that I learn to love the brothers with his own love.

Blood and Water

"They shall look on him whom they have pierced." Let us look with trust at the pierced side of Jesus from which flow "blood and water" (Jn 19:34)! The Fathers of the Church considered these elements as symbols of the Sacraments of Baptism and the Eucharist. Through the water of Baptism, thanks to the action of the Holy Spirit, we are given access to the intimacy of Trinitarian love. In the Lenten journey, memorial of our Baptism, we are exhorted to come out of ourselves in order to open ourselves in trustful abandonment to the merciful embrace of the Father (cf. St. John Chrysostom, *Catecheses*, 3, 14ff.). Blood, symbol of the love of the Good Shepherd, flows into us especially in the Eucharistic mystery: "The Eucharist draws us into Jesus' act of self-oblation . . . we enter into the very dynamic of his self-giving" (Encyclical *Deus Caritas Est*, no. 13). Let us live Lent, then, as a "Eucharistic" time in which,

welcoming the love of Jesus, we learn to spread it around us with every word and deed. Contemplating "him whom they have pierced" moves us in this way to open our hearts to others, recognizing the wounds inflicted upon the dignity of the human person; it moves us in particular to fight every form of contempt for life and human exploitation and to alleviate the tragedies of loneliness and abandonment of so many people. May Lent be for every Christian a renewed experience of God's love given to us in Christ, a love that each day we, in turn, must "re-give" to our neighbor, especially to the one who suffers most and is in need. Only in this way will we be able to participate fully in the joy of Easter. May Mary, Mother of Beautiful Love, guide us in this Lenten journey, a journey of authentic conversion to the love of Christ. I wish you, dear brothers and sisters, a fruitful Lenten journey, imparting with affection to all of you a special Apostolic Blessing.

"Christ Made Himself Poor for You" (2 Corinthians 8:9)

Dear Brothers and Sisters!

1. Each year, Lent offers us a providential opportunity to deepen the meaning and value of our Christian lives, and it stimulates us to rediscover the mercy of God so that we, in turn, become more merciful toward our brothers and sisters. In the Lenten period, the Church makes it her duty to propose some specific tasks that accompany the faithful concretely in this process of interior renewal: these are *prayer*, *fasting* and *almsgiving*. For this year's Lenten Message, I wish to spend some time reflecting on the practice of almsgiving, which represents a specific way to assist those in need and, at the same time, an exercise in self-denial to free us from attachment to worldly goods. The force of attraction to material riches and just how categorical our decision must be not to make of them an idol, Jesus confirms in a resolute way: "You cannot serve God and mammon" (Lk 16:13). Almsgiving helps us to overcome

this constant temptation, teaching us to respond to our neighbor's needs and to share with others whatever we possess through divine goodness. This is the aim of the special collections in favor of the poor, which are promoted during Lent in many parts of the world. In this way, inward cleansing is accompanied by a gesture of ecclesial communion, mirroring what already took place in the early Church. In his Letters, St. Paul speaks of this in regard to the collection for the Jerusalem community (cf. 2 Cor 8-9; Rom 15:25-27).

2. According to the teaching of the Gospel, we are not owners but rather administrators of the goods we possess: these, then, are not to be considered as our exclusive possession, but means through which the Lord calls each one of us to act as a steward of His providence for our neighbor. As the *Catechism of the Catholic Church* reminds us, material goods bear a social value, according to the principle of their universal destination (cf. no. 2404).

In the Gospel, Jesus explicitly admonishes the one who possesses and uses earthly riches only for self. In the face of the multitudes, who, lacking everything, suffer hunger, the words of St. John acquire the tone of a ringing rebuke: "How does God's love abide in anyone who has the world's goods and sees a brother or sister in need and yet refuses to help?" (1 Jn 3:17). In those countries whose population is majority Christian, the call to share is even more urgent, since their responsibility toward the many who suffer poverty and abandonment is even greater. To come to their aid is a duty of justice even prior to being an act of charity.

3. The Gospel highlights a typical feature of Christian almsgiving: it must be hidden: "Do not let your left hand know what your right hand is doing," Jesus asserts, "so that your alms may be done in secret" (Mt 6:3-4). Just a short while before, He said not to boast of one's own good works so as not to risk being deprived of the heavenly reward (cf. Mt 6:1-2). The disciple is to be concerned with God's greater glory. Jesus warns: "In this way, let your light shine before others, so that they may see your good works and give glory to your Father in heaven" (Mt 5:16). Everything, then, must be done for God's glory and not our own. This understanding, dear brothers and sisters, must accompany every gesture of help to our neighbor, avoiding that it becomes a means to make ourselves the center of attention. If, in accomplishing a good deed, we do not have as our goal God's glory and the real well being of our brothers and sisters, looking rather for a return of personal interest or simply of applause, we place ourselves outside of the Gospel vision. In today's world of images, attentive vigilance is required, since this temptation is great. Almsgiving, according to the Gospel, is not mere philanthropy: rather it is a concrete expression of charity, a theological virtue that demands interior conversion to love of God and neighbor, in imitation of Jesus Christ, who, dying on the Cross, gave His entire self for us. How could we not thank God for the many people who silently, far from the gaze of the media world, fulfill, with this spirit, generous actions in support of one's neighbor in difficulty? There is little use in giving one's personal goods to others if it leads to a heart puffed up in vainglory: for this reason, the one, who knows that

God "sees in secret" and in secret will reward, does not seek human recognition for works of mercy.

4. In inviting us to consider almsgiving with a more profound gaze that transcends the purely material dimension, Scripture teaches us that there is more joy in giving than in receiving (cf. Acts 20:35). When we do things out of love, we express the truth of our being; indeed, we have been created not for ourselves but for God and our brothers and sisters (cf. 2 Cor 5:15). Every time when, for love of God, we share our goods with our neighbor in need, we discover that the fullness of life comes from love and all is returned to us as a blessing in the form of peace, inner satisfaction and joy. Our Father in heaven rewards our almsgiving with His joy. What is more: St. Peter includes among the spiritual fruits of almsgiving the forgiveness of sins: "Charity," he writes, "covers a multitude of sins" (1 Pt 4:8). As the Lenten liturgy frequently repeats, God offers to us sinners the possibility of being forgiven. The fact of sharing with the poor what we possess disposes us to receive such a gift. In this moment, my thought turns to those who realize the weight of the evil they have committed and, precisely for this reason, feel far from God, fearful and almost incapable of turning to Him. By drawing close to others through almsgiving, we draw close to God; it can become an instrument for authentic conversion and reconciliation with Him and our brothers.

5. Almsgiving teaches us the generosity of love. St. Joseph Benedict Cottolengo forthrightly recommends, "Never keep an account of the coins you give, since this is what I always say: if, in giving alms, the left hand is not

to know what the right hand is doing, then the right hand, too, should not know what it does itself" (*Detti e pensieri*, Edilibri, no. 201). In this regard, all the more significant is the Gospel story of the widow who, out of her poverty, cast into the Temple treasury "all she had to live on" (Mk 12:44). Her tiny and insignificant coin becomes an eloquent symbol: this widow gives to God not out of her abundance, not so much what she has, but what she is. Her entire self.

We find this moving passage inserted in the description of the days that immediately precede Jesus' passion and death, who, as St. Paul writes, made Himself poor to enrich us out of His poverty (cf. 2 Cor 8:9); He gave His entire self for us. Lent, also through the practice of almsgiving, inspires us to follow His example. In His school, we can learn to make of our lives a total gift; imitating Him, we are able to make ourselves available, not so much in giving a part of what we possess, but our very selves. Cannot the entire Gospel be summarized perhaps in the one commandment of love? The Lenten practice of almsgiving thus becomes a means to deepen our Christian vocation. In gratuitously offering himself, the Christian bears witness that it is love and not material richness that determines the laws of his existence. Love, then, gives almsgiving its value; it inspires various forms of giving, according to the possibilities and conditions of each person.

6. Dear brothers and sisters, Lent invites us to "train ourselves" spiritually, also through the practice of almsgiving, in order to grow in charity and recognize in the poor Christ Himself. In the Acts of the Apostles, we read that the Apostle Peter said to the cripple who was begging alms at

the Temple gate: "I have no silver or gold, but what I have I give you; in the name of Jesus Christ the Nazarene, walk" (Acts 3:6). In giving alms, we offer something material, a sign of the greater gift that we can impart to others through the announcement and witness of Christ, in whose name is found true life. Let this time, then, be marked by a personal and community effort of attachment to Christ in order that we may be witnesses of His love. May Mary, Mother and faithful Servant of the Lord, help believers to enter the "spiritual battle" of Lent, armed with prayer, fasting and the practice of almsgiving, so as to arrive at the celebration of the Easter Feasts, renewed in spirit. With these wishes, I willingly impart to all my Apostolic Blessing.

In the Love of Christ, the Heart of God and the Hearts of Men Touched

Dear Brothers and Sisters,

In his farewell discourse, Jesus announced his imminent death and Resurrection to his disciples with these mysterious words: "I go away, and I will come to you," he said (Jn 14:28). Dying is a "going away." Even if the body of the deceased remains behind, he himself has gone away into the unknown, and we cannot follow him (cf. Jn 13:36). Yet in Jesus's case, there is something utterly new, which changes the world. In the case of our own death, the "going away" is definitive, there is no return. Jesus, on the other hand, says of his death: "I go away, and I will come to you." It is by going away that he comes. His going ushers in a completely new and greater way of being present. By dying he enters into the love of the Father. His dying is an act of love. Love, however, is immortal. Therefore, his going away is transformed into a new coming, into a form of presence which reaches deeper and does not come to an end. During his earthly life, Jesus, like all of us, was tied to the external conditions of bodily existence: to a determined place and a determined time. Bodiliness places limits on our existence. We cannot be simultaneously in two different places. Our time is destined to come to an end. And between the "I" and the "you" there is a wall of otherness. To be sure, through love we can somehow enter the other's existence. Nevertheless, the insurmountable barrier of being different remains in place. Yet Jesus, who is now totally transformed through the act of love, is free from such barriers and limits. He is able not only to pass through closed doors in the outside world, as the Gospels recount (cf. Jn 20:19). He can pass through the interior door separating the "I" from the "you," the closed door between yesterday and today, between the past and the future. On the day of his solemn entry into Jerusalem, when some Greeks asked to see him, Jesus replied with the parable of the grain of wheat which has to pass through death in order to bear much fruit. In this way he foretold his own destiny: these words were not addressed simply to one or two Greeks in the space of a few minutes. Through his Cross, through his going away, through his dying like the grain of wheat, he would truly arrive among the Greeks, in such a way that they could see him and touch him through faith. His going away is transformed into a coming, in the Risen Lord's universal manner of presence, yesterday, today and for ever. He also comes today, and he embraces all times and all places. Now he can even surmount the wall of otherness that separates the "I" from the "you." This happened with

Paul, who describes the process of his conversion and his Baptism in these words: "It is no longer I who live, but Christ who lives in me" (Gal 2:20). Through the coming of the Risen One, Paul obtained a new identity. His closed "I" was opened. Now he lives in communion with Jesus Christ, in the great "I" of believers who have become—as he puts it—"one in Christ" (Gal 3:28).

So, dear friends, it is clear that, through Baptism, the mysterious words spoken by Jesus at the Last Supper become present for you once more. In Baptism, the Lord enters your life through the door of your heart. We no longer stand alongside or in opposition to one another. He passes through all these doors. This is the reality of Baptism: he, the Risen One, comes; he comes to you and joins his life with yours, drawing you into the open fire of his love. You become one, one with him, and thus one among yourselves. At first this can sound rather abstract and unrealistic. But the more you live the life of the baptized, the more you can experience the truth of these words. Believers—the baptized—are never truly cut off from one another. Continents, cultures, social structures or even historical distances may separate us. But when we meet, we know one another on the basis of the same Lord, the same faith, the same hope, the same love, which form us. Then we experience that the foundation of our lives is the same. We experience that in our inmost depths we are anchored in the same identity, on the basis of which all our outward differences, however great they may be, become secondary. Believers are never totally cut off from one another. We are in communion because of our deepest identity: Christ within us.

Thus faith is a force for peace and reconciliation in the world: distances between people are overcome, in the Lord we have become close (cf. Eph 2:13).

The Church expresses the inner reality of Baptism as the gift of a new identity through the tangible elements used in the administration of the sacrament. The fundamental element in Baptism is water; next, in second place, is light, which is used to great effect in the Liturgy of the Easter Vigil. Let us take a brief look at these two elements. In the final chapter of the Letter to the Hebrews, there is a statement about Christ which does not speak directly of water, but the Old Testament allusions nevertheless point clearly to the mystery of water and its symbolic meaning. Here we read: "The God of peace . . . brought again from the dead our Lord Jesus, the great shepherd of the sheep, by the blood of the eternal covenant" (13:20). In this sentence, there is an echo of the prophecy of Isaiah, in which Moses is described as the shepherd whom the Lord brought up from the water, from the sea (cf. 63:11). And Jesus now appears as the new, definitive Shepherd who brings to fulfillment what Moses had done: he leads us out of the deadly waters of the sea, out of the waters of death. In this context we may recall that Moses' mother placed him in a basket in the Nile. Then, through God's providence, he was taken out of the water, carried from death to life, and thus—having himself been saved from the waters of death—he was able to lead others through the sea of death. Jesus descended for us into the dark waters of death. But through his blood, so the Letter to the Hebrews tells us, he was brought back from death: his love united itself to the

Father's love, and thus from the abyss of death he was able to rise to life. Now he raises us from the waters of death to true life. This is exactly what happens in Baptism: he draws us towards himself, he draws us into true life. He leads us through the often murky sea of history, where we are frequently in danger of sinking amid all the confusion and perils. In Baptism he takes us, as it were, by the hand, he leads us along the path that passes through the Red Sea of this life and introduces us to everlasting life, the true and upright life. Let us grasp his hand firmly! Whatever may happen, whatever may befall us, let us not lose hold of his hand! Let us walk along the path that leads to life.

In the second place, there is the symbol of light and fire. Gregory of Tours (fourth century) recounts a practice that in some places was preserved for a long time, of lighting the new fire for the celebration of the Easter Vigil directly from the sun, using a crystal. Light and fire, so to speak, were received anew from heaven, so that all the lights and fires of the year could be kindled from them. This is a symbol of what we are celebrating in the Easter Vigil. Through his radical love for us, in which the heart of God and the heart of man touched, Jesus Christ truly took light from heaven and brought it to the earth—the light of truth and the fire of love that transform man's being. He brought the light, and now we know who God is and what God is like. Thus we also know what our human situation is: what we are, and for what purpose we exist. When we are baptized, the fire of this light is brought down deep within ourselves. Thus, in the early Church, Baptism was also called the Sacrament of Illumination: God's light enters into us; thus we ourselves become children of light. We must not allow this light of truth, that shows us the path, to be extinguished. We must protect it from all the forces that seek to eliminate it so as to cast us back into darkness regarding God and ourselves. Darkness, at times, can seem comfortable. I can hide, and spend my life asleep. Yet we are not called to darkness, but to light. In our baptismal promises, we rekindle this light, so to speak, year by year. Yes, I believe that the world and my life are not the product of chance, but of eternal Reason and eternal Love, they are created by Almighty God. Yes, I believe that in Jesus Christ, in his incarnation, in his Cross and Resurrection, the face of God has been revealed; that in him, God is present in our midst, he unites us and leads us towards our goal, towards eternal Love. Yes, I believe that the Holy Spirit gives us the word of truth and enlightens our hearts; I believe that in the communion of the Church we all become one Body with the Lord, and thus we encounter his Resurrection and eternal life. The Lord has granted us the light of truth. This light is also fire, a powerful force coming from God, a force that does not destroy, but seeks to transform our hearts, so that we truly become men of God, and so that his peace can become active in this world.

In the early Church there was a custom whereby the Bishop or the priest, after the homily, would cry out to the faithful: "*Conversi ad Dominum*"—turn now toward the Lord. This meant in the first place that they would turn toward the East, toward the rising sun, the sign of Christ returning, whom we go to meet when we celebrate the Eucharist. Where this was not possible, for some reason, they would at least turn towards the image of Christ in the apse, or towards the Cross, so as to orient themselves inwardly towards the Lord. Fundamentally, this involved an interior event; *conversion*, the turning of our soul toward Jesus Christ and thus toward the living God, toward the true light. Linked with this, then, was the other exclamation that still today, before the Eucharistic Prayer, is addressed to the community of the faithful: "*Sursum corda*"—"Lift up your hearts," high above all our misguided concerns, desires, anxieties and thoughtlessness— "Lift up your hearts, your inner selves!" In both exclamations we are summoned, as it were, to a renewal of our Baptism: *Conversi ad Dominum*—we must always turn away from false paths, onto which we stray so often in our thoughts and actions. We must turn ever anew toward him who is the Way, the Truth and the Life. We must be converted ever anew, turning with our whole life towards the Lord. And ever anew we must withdraw our hearts from the force of gravity, which pulls them down, and inwardly we must raise them high: in truth and love. At this hour, let us thank the Lord, because through the power of his word and of the holy Sacraments, he points us in the right direction and draws our heart upwards. Let us pray to him in these words: Yes, Lord, make us Easter people, men and women of light, filled with the fire of your love. Amen.

BENEDICT XVI

General Audience
St. Peter's Square
Wednesday, November 5, 2008

The Importance of Christology: The Decisiveness of the Resurrection

Dear Brothers and Sisters,

"If Christ has not been raised, then our preaching is in vain and your faith is in vain . . . and you are still in your sins" (1 Cor 15:14-17). With these strong words from the First Letter to the Corinthians, St. Paul makes clear the decisive importance he attributes to the Resurrection of Jesus. In this event, in fact, lies the solution to the problem posed by the drama of the Cross. The Cross alone could not explain the Christian faith, indeed it would remain a tragedy, an indication of the absurdity of being. The Paschal Mystery consists in the fact that the Crucified man "was raised on the third day, in accordance with the Scriptures" (1 Cor 15:4), as proto-Christian tradition attests. This is the keystone of Pauline Christology: everything rotates around this gravitational center. The whole teaching of Paul the Apostle starts *from*, and arrives *at*, the mystery of him whom the Father raised from the dead. The Resurrection is a fundamental fact, almost a prior axiom (cf. 1 Cor 15:12), on the basis of which Paul can formulate his synthetic proclamation (*kerygma*). He who was crucified and who thus manifested God's immense love for man, is risen again, and is alive among us.

It is important to understand the relationship between the proclamation of the Resurrection, as Paul formulates it, and that was in use since the first pre-Pauline Christian communities. Here indeed we can see the importance of the tradition that preceded the Apostle and that he, with great respect and care, desires to pass on in his turn. The text on the Resurrection, contained in chapter 15:1-11 of the First Letter to the Corinthians, emphasizes the connection between "receiving" and "transmitting." St. Paul attributes great importance to the literal formulation of the tradition, and at the end of the passage under consideration underlines, "What matters is that I preach what they preach" (1 Cor 15:11), so drawing attention to the oneness of the *kerygma*, of the proclamation for all believers and for those who will proclaim the Resurrection of Christ. The *tradition* to which he refers is the fount from which to draw. His Christology is never original at the expense of faithfulness to tradition. The *kerygma* of the Apostles always presides over the personal re-elaboration of Paul; each of his arguments moves from common tradition, and in them he expresses the faith shared by all the Churches, which are one single Church. In this way St. Paul offers a model for all time of how to approach theology and how to preach. The theologian, the preacher, does not create new visions of the world and of life, but he is at the service of truth handed down, at the service of the real fact of Christ, of the Cross, and of the Resurrection. His task is to help us understand today the reality of "God with us" that lies behind the ancient words, and thus the reality of true life.

We should here be explicit: St. Paul, in proclaiming the Resurrection, does not worry about presenting an organic doctrinal exposition—he does not wish to write what would effectively be a theological handbook—but he approaches the theme by replying to doubts and concrete questions asked of him by the faithful; an unprepared discourse, then, but one full of faith and theological experience. We find here a concentration of the essential: we have been "justified," that is made just, saved, by Christ who *died* and *rose* again for us. Above all else the *fact* of the Resurrection emerges, without which Christian life would be simply in vain. On that Easter morning something extraordinary happened, something new, and at the same time very concrete, distinguished by very precise signs and recorded by numerous witnesses. For Paul, as for the other authors of the New Testament, the Resurrection is closely bound to the *testimony* of those who had direct experience of the Risen One. This means seeing and hearing, not only with the eyes or with the senses, but also with an interior light that assists the recognition of what the external senses attest as objective fact.

Paul gives, therefore, as do the four Gospels, primary importance to the theme of the *appearances*, which constitute a fundamental condition for belief in the Risen One who left the tomb empty. These two facts are important:

the tomb is empty and *Jesus has in fact appeared*. In this way the links of that tradition were forged, which, through the testimony of the Apostles and the first disciples, was to reach successive generations until it came down to our own. The first consequence, or the first way of expressing this testimony, is to preach the Resurrection of Christ as a synthesis of the Gospel proclamation and as the culminating point in the salvific itinerary. Paul does all this on many occasions: looking at the Letters and the Acts of the Apostles, we can see that for him the essential point is to bear witness to the Resurrection. I should like to cite just one text: Paul, arrested in Jerusalem, stands accused before the Sanhedrin. In this situation, where his life is at stake, he indicates what is the sense and content of all his preaching: "With respect to the hope and the resurrection of the dead I am on trial" (Acts 23:6). This same phrase Paul continually repeats in his Letters (cf. 1 Thes 1:9ff.; 4:13-18; 5:10), in which he refers to his own personal experience, to his own meeting with the Risen Christ (cf. Gal 1:15-16, 1 Cor 9:1).

But we may wonder, what, for St. Paul, is the deep meaning of the Resurrection of Jesus? What has he to say to us across these 2,000 years? Is the affirmation "Christ is risen" relevant to us today? Why is the Resurrection so important, both for him and for us? Paul gives a solemn answer to this question at the beginning of his Letter to the Romans, where he begins by referring to "the Gospel of God . . . concerning his Son, who was descended from David according to the flesh, and designated Son of God in power according to the spirit of holiness by his resurrection from the dead" (Rom 1:3-4). Paul knows well, and often says, that Jesus was always the Son of God, from the moment of his Incarnation. The novelty of the Resurrection consists in the fact that Jesus, raised from the lowliness of his earthly existence, is constituted Son of God "in power." Jesus, humiliated up to the moment of his death on the Cross, can now say to the Eleven, "All authority in heaven and on earth has been given to me" (Mt 28:18). The affirmation of Psalm 2:8 has come to pass: "Ask of me, and I will make the nations your heritage, and the ends of the earth your possession." So, with the Resurrection begins the proclamation of the Gospel of Christ to all peoples—the Kingdom of Christ begins, this new Kingdom that knows no power other than that of truth and love. The Resurrection thus reveals definitively the real identity and the extraordinary stature of the Crucified One. An incomparable and towering dignity: *Jesus is God!* For St. Paul, the secret identity of Jesus is revealed even more in the mystery of the Resurrection than in the Incarnation. *While the title of Christ*, that is "Messiah"; "the Anointed," in St. Paul tends to become the proper name of Jesus, and that of "*the Lord*" indicates his personal relationship with believers, now the title "*Son of God*" comes to illustrate the intimate relationship of Jesus with God, a relationship which is fully revealed in the Paschal event. We can say, therefore, that Jesus rose again to be the Lord of the living and the dead (cf. Rom 14:9; and 2 Cor 5:15), or in other words, our Savior (cf. Rom 4:25).

All this bears important consequences for our lives as believers: we are called upon to take part, in our inmost selves, in the whole story of the death and Resurrection of Christ. The Apostle says: We "have died with Christ" and we believe we shall "live with him. For we know that Christ being raised from the dead, will never die again; death no longer has dominion over him" (Rom 6:8-9). This means sharing in the suffering of Christ, which is a prelude to that full unity with him through the resurrection that we hope for. This is also what happened to St. Paul, whose personal experience is described in the Letters in tones as sorrowful as they are realistic: "That I may know him and the power of his Resurrection, and may share his sufferings becoming like him in his death, that if possible I may attain the resurrection from the dead" (Phil 3:10-11; cf. 2 Tm 2:8-12). The theology of the Cross is not a theory—it is the reality of Christian life. To live in the belief in Jesus Christ, to live in truth and love implies daily sacrifice, implies suffering. Christianity is not the easy road; it is, rather, a difficult climb, but one illuminated by the light of Christ and by the great hope that is born of him. St. Augustine says: Christians are not spared suffering, indeed they must suffer a little more, because to live the faith expresses the courage to face in greater depth the problems that life and history present. But only in this way, through the experience of suffering, can we know life in its profundity, in its beauty, in the great hope born from Christ crucified and risen again. The believer, however, finds himself between two poles: on the one hand, the Resurrection, which in a certain sense is already present and operating within us (cf. Col 3:1-4; Eph 2:6); on the other, the urgency to enter into the process which leads everyone and everything toward that fullness described in the Letter to the Romans with a bold image:

as the whole of Creation groans and suffers almost as with the pangs of childbirth, so we groan in the expectation of the redemption of our bodies, of our redemption and resurrection (cf. Rom 8:18-23).

In synthesis, we can say with Paul that the true believer obtains salvation by professing with his mouth that Jesus is the *Lord* and believing in his heart that *God has raised Him from the dead* (cf. Rom 10:9). Important above all else is the heart that believes in Christ, and which in its faith "touches" the Risen One; but it is not enough to carry our faith in our heart, we must confess it and bear witness to it with our mouths, with our lives, thus making the truth of the Cross and the Resurrection present in our history. In this way the Christian becomes part of that process by which the first Adam, a creature of the earth, and subject to corruption and death, is transformed into the last Adam, heavenly and incorruptible (cf. 1 Cor 15:20-22 and 42-49). This process was set in motion by the Resurrection of Christ, and it is, therefore, on this that we found our hope that we too may one day enter with Christ into our true homeland, which is in Heaven. Borne up by this hope, let us continue with courage and with joy.

To the Participants at the Meeting
Promoted by the Pontifical Council "Cor Unum"
Sala Clementina
Monday, January 23, 2006

In My First Encyclical, the Themes "God," "Christ" and "Love" Are Fused Together as the Central Guide of Christian Faith

Your Eminences,
Your Excellencies,
Ladies and Gentlemen,

The cosmic excursion in which Dante, in his "Divine Comedy," wishes to involve the reader, ends in front of the perennial Light that is God himself, before that Light which is at the same time "*the love that moves the sun and the other stars*" (Par. XXXIII, v. 145). Light and love are one and the same. They are the primordial creative powers that move the universe.

If these words in Dante's *Paradiso* betray the thought of Aristotle, who saw in the *eros* the power that moves the world, Dante nevertheless perceives something completely new and inconceivable for the Greek philosopher. Not only that the eternal Light is shown in three circles which Dante addresses using those terse verses familiar to us: *"O everlasting Light, you dwell alone/In yourself, know yourself alone, and known/And knowing, love and smile upon yourself!"* (Par. XXXIII, vv. 124-126).

As a matter of fact, even more overwhelming than this revelation of God as a trinitarian circle of knowledge and love, is the perception of a human face—the face of Jesus Christ—which, to Dante, appears in the central circle of the Light. God, infinite Light, whose immeasurable mystery the Greek philosopher perceived, this God has a human face and—we may add—a human heart.

This vision of Dante reveals, on the one hand, the continuity between Christian faith in God and the search developed by reason and by the world of religions; on the other, however, a novelty appears that surpasses all human research, the novelty that only God himself can reveal to us: the novelty of a love that moved God to take on a human face, even to take on flesh and blood, the entire human being.

The *eros* of God is not only a primordial cosmic power; it is love that created man and that bows down over him, as the Good Samaritan bent down to the wounded and robbed man, lying on the side of the road that went down from Jerusalem to Jericho.

Today, the word "love" is so spoiled, worn out and abused that one almost fears to pronounce it. And yet, it is a fundamental word, an expression of the primordial reality. We cannot simply abandon it, but we must take it up again, purify it and bring it to its original splendor so that it can illumine our life and guide it on the right path.

This is the understanding that led me to choose "love" as the theme of my first Encyclical. I wanted to try to express for our time and our existence some of what Dante boldly summed up in his vision. He tells of a "*sight*" that "*was altering*" as he "gazed on" it and was being interiorly changed (cf. Par. XXXIII, vv. 112-114).

It is precisely this: faith becomes a vision-understanding that transforms us. It was my aim to shed light on the centrality of faith in God; in that God who took on a human face and heart.

Faith is not a theory that can be personalized or even set aside. It is something very concrete: it is the criterion that determines our lifestyle. In an epoch where hostility and greed have become superpowers, an epoch where we support the abuse of religion to the point of deifying hatred, neutral rationality alone cannot protect us. We need the living God, who loved us even to death. And so, in this Encyclical, the themes "God," "Christ" and "Love" are fused together as the central guide of Christian faith. I wanted to reveal the humanity of faith, of which *eros* is a part; the "yes" of man to his bodiliness created by God, a "yes" that in an indissoluble matrimony between man and woman finds its form rooted in creation.

And here it also happens that the *eros* is transformed into *agape*: that love for the other which is no longer self-seeking but becomes concern for the other, ready to sacrifice for him or her and also open to the gift of a new human life.

Christian *agape*, love of neighbor in the following of Christ, is nothing foreign to, situated alongside of or even against the *eros*; on the contrary, in the sacrifice that Christ made of himself for man he discovered a new dimension which, in the history of charitable dedication of Christians to the poor and suffering, it has developed all the more.

A first reading of the Encyclical could possibly give the impression that it is divided into two parts that are not very connected: a first part, theoretical, which speaks about the essence of love, and a second, which speaks of ecclesial charity and charitable organizations.

I was particularly interested, however, in the unity of the two themes that are well understood only if seen as a whole. From the beginning it was necessary to speak of the essence of love as it is presented to us in the light of biblical testimony. Starting from the Christian image of God, it was necessary to show how man is created for love and how this love, which initially appears above all as the *eros* between man and woman, must then be interiorly transformed into *agape*, into gift of self to the other; and this, precisely to respond to the true nature of the *eros*.

On this basis, then, the essence of the love of God and neighbor as described in the Bible is shown to be the center of Christian existence, the result of faith.

Subsequently, however, in the second part it became necessary to stress that the totally personal act of *agape* can never remain as something isolated, but must instead become also an essential act of the Church as community: meaning that it also requires an institutional form which is expressed in the communal working of the Church.

The ecclesial organization of charity is not a form of social assistance that is casually added to the Church's reality, an initiative that could also be left to others. Instead, it is part of the nature of the Church.

As the divine *Logos* corresponds to the human announcement, the word of faith, so must the *Agape*, who is God, correspond to the *agape* of the Church, her charitable activity. This activity, beyond the first very concrete meaning of helping one's neighbor, also essentially means that of communicating to others God's love, which we ourselves have received. It must make the living God in some way visible.

In charitable organization, God and Christ must not be foreign words; in reality, they indicate the original source of ecclesial charity. The strength of *Caritas* depends on the strength of the faith of all the members and collaborators.

The sight of a suffering human being touches our heart. But charitable commitment has a meaning that goes well beyond simple philanthropy. It is God himself who moves us interiorly to relieve misery. And so, after all, it is he himself whom we bring to the suffering world.

The more consciously and clearly we bring him as a gift, the more effectively will our love change the world and reawaken hope: a hope that goes beyond death. And only in this way is it true hope for man.

I hope that the Lord will bless your Symposium.

Christ and the Church

Dear Brothers and Sisters,

Following the Catecheses on the Psalms and Canticles of Lauds and of Vespers, I would like to dedicate the upcoming Wednesday Audiences to the mystery of the relationship between Christ and the Church, reflecting upon it from the experience of the Apostles, in light of the duty entrusted to them.

The Church was built on the foundation of the Apostles as a community of faith, hope and charity. Through the Apostles, we come to Jesus himself. The Church begins to establish herself when some fishermen of Galilee meet Jesus, allowing themselves to be won over by his gaze, his voice, his warm and strong invitation: "Follow me, and I will make you become fishers of men" (Mk 1:17; Mt 4:19).

At the start of the third millennium, my beloved Predecessor John Paul II invited the Church to contemplate the Face of Christ (cf. *Novo Millennio Ineunte*, no. 16 ff.). Continuing in the same direction, I would like to show, in the Catechesis that I begin today, how it is precisely the light of that Face that is reflected on the face of the Church (cf. *Lumen Gentium*, no. 1), notwithstanding the limits and shadows of our fragile and sinful humanity.

After Mary, a pure reflection of the light of Christ, it is from the Apostles, through their word and witness, that we receive the truth of Christ. Their mission is not isolated, however, but is situated within a mystery of communion that involves the entire People of God and is carried out in stages from the Old to the New Covenant.

In this regard, it must be said that the message of Jesus is completely misunderstood if it is separated from the context of the faith and hope of the Chosen People: like John the Baptist, his direct Precursor, Jesus above all addresses Israel (cf. Mt 15:24) in order to "gather" it together in the eschatological time that arrived with him. And like that of John, the preaching of Jesus is at the same time a call of grace and a sign of contradiction and of justice for the entire People of God.

And so, from the first moment of his salvific activity, Jesus of Nazareth strives to gather together the People of God. Even if his preaching is always an appeal for personal conversion, in reality he continually aims to build the People of God whom he came to bring together, purify and save.

As a result, therefore, an individualistic interpretation of Christ's proclamation of the Kingdom, specific to liberal theology, is unilateral and without foundation, as a great liberal theologian Adolf von Harnack summed it up in the year 1900 in his lessons on *The Essence of Christianity*: "The Kingdom of God, insofar as it comes in *single* individuals, is able to enter their soul and is welcomed by them. The Kingdom of God is the *dominion* of God, certainly, but it is the dominion of the holy God in individual hearts" (cf. Third Lesson, 100 ff.).

In reality, this individualism of liberal theology is a typically modern accentuation: in the perspective of biblical tradition and on the horizon of Judaism, where the work of Jesus is situated in all its novelty, it is clear that the entire mission of the Son-made-flesh has a communitarian finality. He truly came to unite dispersed humanity; he truly came to unite the People of God.

An evident sign of the intention of the Nazarene to gather together the community of the Covenant, to demonstrate in it the fulfillment of the promises made to the Fathers who always speak of convocation, unification, unity, is *the institution of the Twelve*. We heard about this institution of the Twelve in the Gospel reading. I shall read the central passage again: "And he went up into the hills and called to him those whom he desired; and they came to him. And he appointed twelve to be with him, and to be sent out to preach and have authority to cast out demons. The names of the twelve Apostles are these . . . " (Mk 3:13-16; cf. Mt 10:1-4; Lk 6:12-16).

On the site of the revelation, "the mount," taking initiative that demonstrates absolute awareness and determination, Jesus establishes the Twelve so that, together with him, they are witnesses and heralds of the coming of the Kingdom of God.

There are no doubts about the historicity of this call, not only because of the antiquity and multiplicity of witnesses, but also for the simple reason that there is also the name of Judas, the Apostle who betrayed him, notwithstanding the difficulties that this presence could have caused the new community.

The number twelve, which evidently refers to the twelve tribes of Israel, already reveals the meaning of the prophetic-symbolic action implicit in the new initiative to re-establish the holy people. As the system of the twelve tribes had long since faded out, the hope of Israel awaited their restoration as a sign of the eschatological time (as referred to at the end of the Book of Ezekiel: 37:15-19; 39:23-29; 40-48).

In choosing the Twelve, introducing them into a communion of life with himself and involving them in his mission of proclaiming the Kingdom in words and works (cf. Mk 6:7-13; Mt 10:5-8; Lk 9:1-6; 6:13), Jesus wants to say that the definitive time has arrived in which to constitute the new People of God, the people of the twelve tribes, which now becomes a universal people, his Church.

Appeal for Israel

With their very own existence, the Twelve—called from different backgrounds—become an appeal for all of Israel to convert and allow herself to be gathered into the new covenant, complete and perfect fulfillment of the ancient one. The fact that he entrusted to his Apostles, during the Last Supper and before his Passion, the duty to celebrate his Pasch, demonstrates how Jesus wished to transfer to the entire community, in the person of its heads, the mandate to be a sign and instrument in history of the eschatological gathering begun by him. In a certain sense we can say that the Last Supper itself is the act of foundation of the Church, because he gives himself and thus creates a new community, a community united in communion with himself.

In this light, one understands how the Risen One confers upon them, with the effusion of the Spirit, the power to forgive sins (cf. Jn 20:23). Thus, the Twelve Apostles are the most evident sign of Jesus' will regarding the existence and mission of his Church, the guarantee that between Christ and the Church there is no opposition: despite the sins of the people who make up the Church, they are inseparable.

Therefore, a slogan that was popular some years back: "Jesus yes, Church no," is totally inconceivable with the intention of Christ. This individualistically chosen Jesus is an imaginary Jesus.

We cannot have Jesus without the reality he created and in which he communicates himself. Between the Son of God-made-flesh and his Church there is a profound, unbreakable and mysterious continuity by which Christ is present today in his people. He is always contemporary with us, he is always contemporary with the Church, built on the foundation of the Apostles and alive in the succession of the Apostles. And his very presence in the community, in which he himself is always with us, is the reason for our joy. Yes, Christ is with us, the Kingdom of God is coming.

St. Paul and the Church

Dear Brothers and Sisters,

Today, we are ending our encounters with the Apostle Paul by dedicating one last reflection to him. Indeed, we cannot take our leave of him without considering one of the decisive elements of his activity and one of the most important subjects of his thought: the reality of the Church.

We must first of all note that his initial contact with the Person of Jesus happened through the witness of the Christian community of Jerusalem. It was a turbulent contact. Having met the new group of believers, he immediately became a fierce persecutor of it. He acknowledged this himself at least three times in as many of his Letters: "I persecuted the Church of God" (1 Cor 15:9; Gal 1:13; Phil 3:6), as if to describe his behavior as the worst possible crime.

History shows us that one usually reaches Jesus by passing through the Church! In a certain sense, this proved true, we were saying, also for Paul, who encountered the Church before he encountered Jesus. In his case, however, this contact was counterproductive; it did not result in attachment but violent rejection.

For Paul, adherence to the Church was brought about by a direct intervention of Christ, who in revealing himself on the road to Damascus identified himself with the Church and made Paul realize that persecution of the Church was persecution of himself, the Lord.

In fact, the Risen One said to Paul, persecutor of the Church: "Saul, Saul, why do you persecute me?" (Acts 9:4). In persecuting the Church, he was persecuting Christ.

Paul, therefore, was at the same time converted to Christ and to the Church. This leads one to understand why the Church later became so present in Paul's thoughts, heart and activity.

In the first place, she was so present that he literally founded many Churches in the various cities where he went as an evangelizer. When he spoke of his "anxiety for all the Churches" (2 Cor 11:28), he was thinking of the various Christian communities brought into being from time to time in Galatia, Ionia, Macedonia and in Achaea.

Some of those Churches also caused him worry and chagrin, as happened, for example, in the Churches of Galatia, which he saw "turning to a different gospel" (Gal 1:6), something he opposed with grim determination.

Yet, he felt bound to the Communities he founded in a way that was far from cold and bureaucratic but rather intense and passionate. Thus, for example, he described the Philippians as "my brethren, whom I love and long for, my joy and crown" (Phil 4:1).

On other occasions he compared the various Communities to a letter of recommendation, unique in its kind: "You yourselves are our letter of recommendation, written on your hearts, to be known and read by all men" (2 Cor 3:2).

At yet other times, he showed a real feeling for them that was not only paternal but also maternal, such as when he turned to those he was addressing, calling them: "My little children, with whom I am again in travail until Christ be formed in you" (Gal 4:19; cf. also 1 Cor 4:14-15; 1 Thes 2:7-8).

Paul also illustrates for us in his Letters his teaching on the Church as such. Thus, his original definition of the Church as the "Body of Christ," which we do not find in other Christian authors of the first century, is well known (cf. 1 Cor 12:27; Eph 4:12; 5:30; Col 1:24).

We find the deepest root of this surprising designation of the Church in the Sacrament of the Body of Christ. St. Paul said: "Because there is one bread, we who are many are one body" (1 Cor 10:17). In the same Eucharist, Christ gives us his Body and makes us his Body. Concerning this, St. Paul said to the Galatians: "You are all one in Christ" (Gal 3:28). By saying all this, Paul makes us understand that not only does the belonging of the Church to Christ exist, but also a certain form of equality and identification of the Church with Christ himself.

From this, therefore, derive the greatness and nobility of the Church, that is, of all of us who are part of her: from our being members of Christ, an extension as it were of his personal presence in the world. And from this, of course, stems our duty to truly live in conformity with Christ.

Paul's exhortations concerning the various charisms that give life and structure to the Christian community also derive from this. They can all be traced back to a single source, that is, the Spirit of the Father and of the Son, knowing well that in the Church there is no one who goes without them, for, as the Apostle wrote, "to each is given the manifestation of the Spirit for the common good" (1 Cor 12:7).

It is important, however, that all the charisms cooperate with one another for the edification of the community and do not instead become the cause of a rift.

In this regard, Paul asked himself rhetorically: "Is Christ divided?" (1 Cor 1:13). He knows well and teaches us that it is necessary to "maintain the unity of the Spirit in the bond of peace. There is one body and one Spirit, just as you were called to the one hope that belongs to your call" (Eph 4:3-4).

Obviously, underlining the need for unity does not mean that ecclesial life should be standardized or leveled out in accordance with a single way of operating. Elsewhere, Paul taught: "Do not quench the Spirit" (1 Thes 5:19), that is, make room generously for the unforeseeable dynamism of the charismatic manifestations of the Spirit, who is an ever new source of energy and vitality.

But if there is one tenet to which Paul stuck firmly it was mutual edification: "Let all things be done for edification" (1 Cor 14:26). Everything contributes to weaving the ecclesial fabric evenly, not only without slack patches but also without holes or tears.

Then, there is also a Pauline Letter that presents the Church as Christ's Bride (cf. Eph 5:21-33).

With this, Paul borrowed an ancient prophetic metaphor which made the People of Israel the Bride of the God of the Covenant (cf. Hos 2:4, 21; Is 54:5-8). He did so to express the intimacy of the relationship between Christ and his Church, both in the sense that she is the object of the most tender love on the part of her Lord, and also in the sense that love must be mutual and that we too therefore, as members of the Church, must show him passionate faithfulness.

Thus, in short, a relationship of communion is at stake: the so to speak *vertical* communion between Jesus Christ and all of us, but also the *horizontal* communion between all who are distinguished in the world by the fact that they "call on the name of Our Lord Jesus Christ" (1 Cor 1:2).

This is our definition: we belong among those who call on the Name of the Lord Jesus Christ. Therefore, we clearly understand how desirable it is that what Paul himself was hoping for when he wrote to the Corinthians should come to pass: "If an unbeliever or an uninitiated enters while all are uttering prophecy, he will be taken to task by all and called to account by all, and the secret of his heart will be laid bare. Falling prostrate, he will worship God, crying out, 'God is truly among you'" (1 Cor 14:24-25).

Our liturgical encounters should be like this. A non-Christian who enters one of our assemblies ought finally to be able to say: "God is truly with you." Let us pray to the Lord to be like this, in communion with Christ and in communion among ourselves.

Ordination of Fifteen Priests
St. Peter's Basilica
Sunday, May 7, 2006

"I Am the Door": It Is Through Christ That One Must Enter the Service of Shepherd

Dear Brothers and Sisters,
Dear Ordinandi,

At this hour, dear friends, when you are being introduced as shepherds in the service of the Great Shepherd, Jesus Christ, through the Sacrament of Orders, it is the Lord himself who, in the Gospel, speaks of serving God's flock.

The image of the shepherd comes from remote times. In the Orient of antiquity, kings would designate themselves as the shepherds of their peoples. Moses and David in the Old Testament, before being called to become the leaders and pastors of the People of God, were in fact shepherds with flocks.

In the anguish of the period of the Exile, confronted by the failure of Israel's shepherds, that is, of its political and religious leaders, Ezekiel sketched the image of God himself as the Shepherd of his people. Through the prophet

God says: "As a shepherd seeks out his flock . . . so will I seek out my sheep; and I will rescue them from all places where they have been scattered on a day of clouds and thick darkness" (Ez 34:12).

Jesus now proclaims that this time has come: he himself is the Good Shepherd through whom God himself cares for his creature, man, gathering human beings and leading them to the true pasture.

St. Peter, whom the Risen Lord charged to tend his sheep, to become a shepherd with him and for him, described Jesus as the "*archipoimen*"—"Chief Shepherd" (cf. 1 Pt 5:4), and by this he meant that it is only possible to be a shepherd of the flock of Jesus Christ through him and in very close communion with him.

The Sacrament of Ordination expresses this very point: through the Sacrament the priest is totally inserted into Christ, so that by starting from him and acting in his sight he may carry out in communion with him the service of Jesus, the one Shepherd, in whom God, as man, wants to be our Shepherd.

The Gospel we have heard this Sunday is only a part of Jesus' great discourse on shepherds. In this passage, the Lord tells us three things about the true shepherd: he gives his own life for his sheep; he knows them and they know him; he is at the service of unity.

Before reflecting on these three characteristics essential to shepherds, it might be useful to recall briefly the previous part of the discourse on shepherds in which Jesus, before designating himself as the Shepherd, says, to our surprise: "I am the door" (Jn 10:7).

It is through him that one must enter the service of shepherd. Jesus highlights very clearly this basic condition by saying: "He who . . . climbs in by another way, that man is a thief and a robber" (Jn 10:1). This word "climbs"— *anabainei* in Greek—conjures up the image of someone climbing over a fence to get somewhere out of bounds to him.

"To climb"—here too we can also see the image of careerism, the attempt to "get ahead," to gain a position through the Church: to make use of and not to serve. It is the image of a man who wants to make himself important, to become a person of note through the priesthood; the image of someone who has as his aim his own exaltation and not the humble service of Jesus Christ.

But the only legitimate ascent towards the shepherd's ministry is the Cross. This is the true way to rise; this is the true door. It is not the desire to become "someone" for oneself, but rather to exist for others, for Christ, and thus through him and with him to be there for the people he seeks, whom he wants to lead on the path of life.

One enters the priesthood through the Sacrament, and this means precisely: through the gift of oneself to Christ, so that he can make use of me; so that I may serve him and follow his call, even if it proves contrary to my desire for self-fulfillment and esteem.

Entering by the door which is Christ means knowing and loving him more and more, so that our will may be united with his will, our action become one with his action.

Dear friends, let us pray ever anew for this intention, let us strive precisely for this: in other words, for Christ to grow within us and for our union with him to become ever deeper, so that through us it is Christ himself who tends the flock.

Let us now take a closer look at the three fundamental affirmations of Jesus on the good shepherd. The first one, which very forcefully pervades the whole discourse on shepherds, says: the shepherd lays down his life for the sheep. The mystery of the Cross is at the center of Jesus' service as a shepherd: it is the great service that he renders to all of us.

He gives himself and not only in a distant past. In the Holy Eucharist he does so every day, he gives himself through our hands, he gives himself to us. For this good reason the Holy Eucharist, in which the sacrifice of Jesus on the Cross remains continually present, truly present among us, is rightly at the center of priestly life.

And with this as our starting point, we also learn what celebrating the Eucharist properly means: it is an encounter with the Lord, who strips himself of his divine glory for our sake, allows himself be humiliated to the point of death on the Cross and thus gives himself to each one of us.

The daily Eucharist is very important for the priest. In it he exposes himself ever anew to this mystery; ever anew he puts himself in God's hands, experiencing at the same time the joy of knowing that He is present, receives me, ever anew raises and supports me, gives me his hand, himself. The Eucharist must become for us a school of life in which we learn to give our lives.

Free for God

Life is not only given at the moment of death and not only in the manner of martyrdom. We must give it day by day. Day after day it is necessary to learn that I do not possess my life for myself. Day by day I must learn to abandon myself; to keep myself available for whatever he, the Lord, needs of me at a given moment, even if other things seem more appealing and more important to me: it means giving life, not taking it.

It is in this very way that we experience freedom: freedom from ourselves, the vastness of being. In this very way, by being useful, in being a person whom the world needs, our life becomes important and beautiful. Only those who give up their own life find it.

Secondly the Lord tells us: "I know my own [sheep] and my own [sheep] know me, as the Father knows me and I know the Father" (Jn 10:14-15).

Here, two apparently quite different relationships are interwoven in this phrase: the relationship between Jesus and the Father and the relationship between Jesus and the people entrusted to him. Yet both these relationships go together, for in the end people belong to the Father and are in search of the Creator, of God.

When they realize that someone is speaking only in his own name and drawing from himself alone, they guess that he is too small and cannot be what they are seeking; but wherever another's voice re-echoes in a person, the voice of the Creator, of the Father, the door opens to the relationship for which the person is longing.

Consequently, this is how it must be in our case. First of all, in our hearts we must live the relationship with Christ and, through him, with the Father; only then can we truly understand people, only in the light of God can the depths of man be understood. Then those who are listening to us realize that we are not speaking of ourselves or of some thing, but of the true Shepherd.

Obviously, Jesus' words also contain the entire practical pastoral task, caring for men and women, going to seek them out, being open to their needs and questions.

Obviously, practical, concrete knowledge of the people entrusted to me is fundamental, and obviously, it is important to understand this way of "knowing" others in the biblical sense: there is no true knowledge without love, without an inner relationship and deep acceptance of the other.

The shepherd cannot be satisfied with knowing names and dates. His way of knowing his sheep must always also be knowing with the heart.

However, it is only possible to do this properly if the Lord has opened our hearts; if our knowing does not bind people to our own small, private self, to our own small heart, but rather makes them aware of the Heart of Jesus, the Heart of the Lord. It must be knowing with the Heart of Jesus, oriented to him, a way of knowing that does not bind the person to me but guides him or her to Jesus, thereby making one free and open. And in this way we too will become close to men and women.

Let us always pray to the Lord anew that we may be granted this way of knowing with the Heart of Jesus, of not binding to me but of binding to the Heart of Jesus and thereby creating a true community.

Lastly, the Lord speaks to us of the service of unity that is entrusted to the shepherd: "I have other sheep that are not of this fold; I must bring them also, and they will heed my voice. So there will be one flock, one shepherd" (Jn 10:16).

John repeated the same thing after the Sanhedrin had decided to kill Jesus, when Caiaphas said that it would be better for the people that one man die for them rather than the entire nation perish. John recognized these words of Caiaphas as prophetic, adding: "Jesus should die for the nation, and not for the nation only, but to gather into one the children of God who are scattered abroad" (11:52).

The relationship between the Cross and unity is revealed: the Cross is the price of unity. Above all, however, it is the universal horizon of Jesus' action that emerges.

If, in his prophecy about the shepherd, Ezekiel was aiming to restore unity among the dispersed tribes of Israel (cf. Ez 34:22-24), here it is a question not only of the unification of a dispersed Israel but of the unification of all the children of God, of humanity—of the Church of Jews and of pagans.

Jesus' mission concerns all humanity. Therefore, the Church is given responsibility for all humanity, so that it may recognize God, the God who for all of us was made man in Jesus Christ, suffered, died and was raised.

The Church must never be satisfied with the ranks of those whom she has reached at a certain point or say that others are fine as they are: Muslims, Hindus and so forth. The Church can never retreat comfortably to within the limits of her own environment. She is charged with universal solicitude; she must be concerned with and for one and all.

We generally have to "translate" this great task in our respective missions. Obviously, a priest, a pastor of souls, must first and foremost be concerned with those who believe and live with the Church, who seek in her their way of life and on their part, like living stones, build the Church, hence, also build and support the priest.

However, we must also—as the Lord says—go out ever anew "to the highways and hedges" (Lk 14:23), to deliver God's invitation to his banquet also to those who have so far heard nothing or have not been stirred within.

This universal service has many forms. One of them is also the commitment to the inner unity of the Church, so that over and above differences and limitations she may be a sign of God's presence in the world, which alone can create this unity.

Among the sculptures of her time, the ancient Church discovered the figure of a shepherd carrying a sheep across his shoulders. Such images may perhaps be part of the idyllic dream of rural life that fascinated the society of that epoch.

For Christians, however, this figure with all its naturalness became the image of the One who set out to seek his lost sheep: humanity; the image of the One who follows us even into our deserts and confusion; the image of the

One who took upon his shoulders the lost sheep, which is humanity, and carried it home.

It has become the image of the true Shepherd, Jesus Christ. Let us entrust ourselves to him. We entrust you to him, dear brothers, especially at this moment, so that he may lead you and carry you all the days of your life; so that he may help you to become, through him and with him, good shepherds of his flock. Amen!

BENEDICT XVI

Meeting with the Bishops of Switzerland
Thursday, November 9, 2006

The Gospel and the Institution Are Inseparable

I would first like to thank you all for this meeting, which seems very important to me as an exercise of collegial affection, an expression of our common responsibility for the Church and for the Gospel in the world at this time. Thank you for everything!

I am sorry that because of other commitments, especially the *ad limina* visits—in these days it is the turn of the German Bishops—I was unable to be with you.

I would have really liked to hear the voice of the Swiss Bishops—but perhaps there will be other opportunities—and of course, also to hear the dialogue of the Roman Curia and the Swiss Bishops: in the Roman Curia too, the Holy Father always speaks as responsible for the whole Church.

Thank you, therefore, for this meeting, which it seems to me is a help to us all because it is an experience of the Church's unity as well as of the hope that accompanies us in all the difficulties that surround us.

In addition, I would like to ask you to excuse me for having come without a prepared text on the very first day;

I had of course given it some thought, but I did not have the time to write. And so, once again now, I am presenting myself with this impoverishment, but it might be right also for a Pope to be poor in all senses at this time in the Church's history.

In any case, I am unable to offer you a grand Discourse now as would have been fitting after a meeting with these results.

I must say, in fact, that I had already read the summary of your discussions and I have listened to it just now with great attention: it seems a very well thought out and rich text. It truly responds to the essential questions that concern us, both for the unity of the Church as a whole and for the specific issues of the Church in Switzerland. It seems to me that it really plots the path for the years to come and demonstrates our common desire to serve the Lord. It is a very rich text.

In reading it, I thought: it would be somewhat absurd if I were now to start once again to treat the topics discussed thoroughly and intensely over the past three days. I see here the condensed and rich result of the work done; to add anything further to the individual points would, I think, be very difficult, partly because the result of the work is known to me but not the actual voices of those who spoke during the discussions.

I therefore thought that perhaps it would be right this evening, at the conclusion, to return once again to the important topics which occupy us and are, in short, the basis of all the details—even if obviously each detail is important.

In the Church, the institution is not merely an external structure while the Gospel is purely spiritual. In fact, the Gospel and the Institution are inseparable because the Gospel has a body, the Lord has a body in this time of ours. Consequently, issues that seem at first sight merely institutional are actually theological and central, because it is a matter of the realization and concretization of the Gospel in our time.

The best thing to do now, therefore, would be to stress once again the great perspectives within which the whole of our reflection takes place. Allow me with the indulgence and generosity of the members of the Roman Curia, to continue in German, because we have excellent interpreters who would otherwise be left idle.

I have thought of two specific themes of which I have already spoken and which I would now like to examine further.

Let us return, therefore, to the subject of "God." The words of St. Ignatius spring to mind: "The Christian is not the result of persuasion, but of power (*Epistula ad Romanos* 3, 3). We should not allow our faith to be drained by too many discussions of multiple, minor details, but rather, should always keep our eyes in the first place on the greatness of Christianity.

I remember, when I used go to Germany in the 1980s and '90s, that I was asked to give interviews and I always knew the questions in advance. They concerned the ordination of women, contraception, abortion and other such constantly recurring problems.

If we let ourselves be drawn into these discussions, the Church is then identified with certain commandments or prohibitions; we give the impression that we are moralists with a few somewhat antiquated convictions, and not even a hint of the true greatness of the faith appears. I therefore consider it essential always to highlight the greatness of our faith—a commitment from which we must not allow such situations to divert us.

In this perspective I would now like to continue by completing last Tuesday's reflections and to stress once again: what matters above all is to tend one's personal relationship with God, with that God who revealed himself to us in Christ.

Augustine repeatedly emphasized the two sides of the Christian concept of God: God is *Logos* and God is *Love*—to the point that he completely humbled himself, assuming a human body and finally, giving himself into our hands as bread. We must always keep in mind and help others to keep in mind these two aspects of the Christian conception of God.

God is *Spiritus Creator*, he is *Logos*, he is reason. And this is why our faith is something that has to do with reason, can be passed on through reason and has no cause to hide from reason, not even from the reason of our age. But precisely this eternal, immeasurable reason is not merely a mathematics of the universe and far less, some *first cause* that withdrew after producing the *Big Bang*.

This reason, on the contrary, has a heart such as to be able to renounce its own immensity and take flesh. And in that alone, to my mind, lies the ultimate, true greatness of our conception of God. We know that God is not a philosophical hypothesis, he is not something that *perhaps* exists, but we know him and he knows us. And we can know him better and better if we keep up a dialogue with him.

This is why it is a fundamental task of pastoral care to teach people how to pray and how to learn to do so personally, better and better. Today, schools of prayer and prayer groups exist; it is obvious that people want them. Many seek meditation elsewhere because they think that they will not be able to find a spiritual dimension in Christianity.

We must show them once again not only that this spiritual dimension exists but that it is the source of all things. To this end, we must increase the number of these schools of prayer, for praying together, where it is possible to learn personal prayer in all its dimensions: as silent listening to God, as a listening that penetrates his Word, penetrates his silence, sounds the depths of his action in history and in one's own person; and to understand his language in one's life and then to learn to respond in prayer with the great prayers of the Psalms of the Old Testament and prayers of the New.

By ourselves, we do not possess words for God, but words have been given to us: the Holy Spirit himself has already formulated words of prayer for us; we can enter them, we can pray with them and thus subsequently, also learn personal prayer ever better; we can "learn" God and thus become sure of him even if he is silent—we can become joyful in God.

This intimate being with God, hence, the experience of God's presence, is what makes us, so to speak, experience ever anew the greatness of Christianity, and then also helps us to find our way through all the trivialities among which, of course, it must also be lived and—day after day, in suffering and loving, in joy and sorrow—put into practice.

And from this viewpoint one perceives, in my opinion, the significance of the Liturgy also as precisely a school of prayer, where the Lord himself teaches us to pray and where we pray together with the Church, both in humble, simple celebrations with only a few of the faithful and also in the feast of faith.

In various conversations, I have perceived now, once again at this very moment, on the one hand, how important for the faithful silence in their contact with God is, and on the other, the feast of faith, how important it is to be able to live festive celebration.

The world also has its feast days. Nietzsche actually said: We can only celebrate if God does not exist. But this is absurd: only if God exists and touches us can there be true festivity. And we know that these feasts of faith open people's hearts wide and create impressions that are helpful for the future. I saw once again during my Pastoral Visits to Germany, Poland and Spain that faith there is lived as a festive celebration and that it accompanies people and guides them.

In this context I would like to mention something else that struck me and made a lasting impression.

In St. Thomas Aquinas' last work that remained unfinished, the *Compendium Theologiae* which he intended to structure simply according to the three theological virtues of faith, hope and charity, the great Doctor began and partly developed his chapter on hope. In it he identified, so to speak, hope with prayer: the chapter on hope is at the same time the chapter on prayer.

Prayer is hope in action. And in fact, true reason is contained in prayer, which is why it is possible to hope: we can come into contact with the Lord of the world, he listens to us, and we can listen to him. This is what St. Ignatius was alluding to and what I wanted to remind you of today, once again: *ou peismones to ergon, alla megethous estin ho Christianismos* (*Ad Rom.* 3, 3)—the truly great thing in Christianity, which does not dispense one from small, daily things but must not be concealed by them either, is this ability to come into contact with God.

The second thing that I have remembered in these very days concerns morals.

I often hear it said that people today have a longing for God, for spirituality, for religion, and are starting once again to see the Church as a possible conversation partner from which, in this regard, they can receive something. (There was a period in which this was basically sought only in other religions.)

Awareness is growing: the Church especially conveys spiritual experience; she is like a tree where the birds can make their nests even if they want to fly away again later— but she is precisely also a place where one can settle for a certain time.

Instead, what people find more difficult is the morality that the Church proclaims. I have pondered on this—I have been pondering on it for a long time—and I see ever more clearly that in our age morality is, as it were, split in two.

Modern society not merely lacks morals but has "discovered" and demands another dimension of morality, which in the Church's proclamation in recent decades and even earlier perhaps has not been sufficiently presented. This dimension includes the great topics of peace, non-violence, justice for all, concern for the poor and respect for creation. They have become an ethical whole which, precisely as a political force, has great power and for many constitutes the substitution or succession of religion.

Instead of religion, seen as metaphysical and as something from above—perhaps also as something individualistic—the great moral themes come into play as the essential which then confers dignity on man and engages him.

This is one aspect: this morality exists and it also fascinates young people, who work for peace, for non-violence, for justice, for the poor, for creation. And there are truly great moral themes that also belong, moreover, to the tradition of the Church. The means offered for their solution, however, are often very unilateral and not always credible, but we cannot dwell on this now. The important topics are present.

The other part of morality, often received controversially by politics, concerns life. One aspect of it is the commitment to life from conception to death, that is, its defense against abortion, against euthanasia, against the manipulation and man's self-authorization in order to dispose of life.

People often seek to justify these interventions with the seemingly great purpose of thereby serving the future generations, and it even appears moral to take human life into one's own hands and manipulate it.

However, on the other hand, the knowledge also exists that human life is a gift that demands our respect and love from the very first to its very last moments, also for the suffering, the disabled and the weak.

The morality of marriage and the family also fit into this context. Marriage is becoming, so to speak, ever more marginalized.

We are aware of the example of certain countries where legislation has been modified so that marriage is no longer defined as a bond between a man and a woman but a bond between persons; with this, obviously, the basic idea is destroyed and society from its roots becomes something quite different.

The awareness that sexuality, *eros* and marriage as a union between a man and a woman go together—"and they become one flesh" (Gn 2:24)—this knowledge is growing weaker and weaker; every type of bond seems entirely normal—they represent a sort of overall morality of non-discrimination and a form of freedom due to man.

Naturally, with this the indissolubility of marriage has become almost a utopian idea which many public figures seem precisely to contradict. So it is that even the family is gradually breaking up.

There are of course many explanations for the problem of the sharp decline in the birth rate, but certainly a decisive role is also played in this by the fact that people want to enjoy life, that they have little confidence in the future and that they feel the family is no longer viable as a lasting community in which future generations may grow up.

In these contexts, therefore, our proclamation clashes with an awareness, as it were, contrary to society and with a sort of anti-morality based on a conception of freedom seen as the faculty to choose autonomously with no pre-defined guidelines, as non-discrimination, hence, as the approval of every type of possibility.

Thus, it autonomously establishes itself as ethically correct, but the other awareness has not disappeared. It exists, and I believe we must commit ourselves to recon-necting these two parts of morality and to making it clear that they must be inseparably united.

Only if human life from conception until death is respected is the ethic of peace possible and credible; only then may non-violence be expressed in every direction, only then can we truly accept creation and only then can we achieve true justice.

I think that this is the great task we have before us: on the one hand, not to make Christianity seem merely morality, but rather a gift in which we are given the love that sustains us and provides us with the strength we need to be able to "lose our own life." On the other hand, in this context of freely given love, we need to move forward toward ways of putting it into practice, whose foundation is always offered to us by the Decalogue, which we must interpret today with Christ and with the Church in a pro-gressive and new way.

These, therefore, were the themes I thought I should and could elaborate. I thank you for your indulgence and your patience. Let us hope that the Lord will help us all on our journey!

BENEDICT XVI

To Members of the Episcopal Conference
of Canada-Ontario
Consistory Hall, Castel Gandolfo
Thursday, September 8, 2006

Make God Visible in the Human Face of Jesus

Your Eminence,
Dear Brother Bishops,

1. "God is love, and he who abides in love abides in God, and God abides in him" (1 Jn 4:16). With fraternal affection I cordially welcome you, the Bishops of Ontario, and I thank Bishop Smith for the kind sentiments expressed on your behalf. I warmly reciprocate them and assure you, and those entrusted to your pastoral care, of my prayers and solicitude. Your visit *ad Limina Apostolorum*, and to the successor of Peter, is an occasion to affirm your commitment to make Christ increasingly more visible within the Church and society, through joyful witness to the Gospel that is Jesus Christ himself.

The Evangelist John's numerous exhortations to abide in the love and truth of Christ evoke an appealing image of a sure and safe dwelling place. God first loves us (1 Jn 4:10) and we, drawn towards this gift, find a resting place where we can "constantly drink anew from the original source, which is Jesus Christ, from whose pierced heart flows the love of God" (*Deus Caritas Est*, no. 7). St. John was also compelled to urge his communities to remain in that love. Already some had been weakened by the disputes and distractions which eventually lead to division.

2. Dear Brothers, your own Diocesan communities are challenged to resonate with the living statement of faith: "We know and believe the love God has for us" (1 Jn 4:16). These words, which eloquently reveal faith as personal adherence to God and concurrent assent to the whole truth that God reveals (cf. *Dominus Iesus*, no. 7), can be credibly proclaimed only in the wake of an encounter with Christ. Drawn by his love the believer entrusts his entire self to God and so becomes one with the Lord (cf. 1 Cor 6:17). In the Eucharist this union is strengthened and renewed by entering into the very dynamic of Christ's self-giving so as to share in the divine life: "He who eats my flesh and drinks my blood abides in me and I in him" (Jn 6:56; cf. *Deus Caritas Est*, no. 13).

St. John's admonition, however, still holds. In increasingly secularized societies such as yours, the Lord's outpouring of love to humanity can remain unnoticed or rejected. By imagining that withdrawing from this relationship is somehow a key to his own liberation, man in fact becomes a stranger to himself, since "in reality it is only in the mystery of the Word made flesh that the mystery of man truly becomes clear" (*Gaudium et Spes*, no. 22). Dismissive of the love which discloses the fullness of man's truth, many men and women continue to walk away from the Lord's abode into a wilderness of individual isolation, social fragmentation and loss of cultural identity.

3. Within this perspective, one sees that the fundamental task of the evangelization of culture is the challenge to make God visible in the human face of Jesus. In helping individuals to recognize and experience the love of Christ, you will awaken in them the desire to dwell in the house of the Lord, embracing the life of the Church. This is our mission. It expresses our ecclesial nature and ensures that every initiative of evangelization concurrently strengthens Christian identity. In this regard, we must acknowledge that any reduction of the core message of Jesus, that is, the "Kingdom of God," to indefinite talk of "kingdom values" weakens Christian identity and debilitates the Church's contribution to the regeneration of society. When believing is replaced by "doing" and witness by talk of "issues," there is an urgent need to recapture the profound joy and awe of the first disciples whose hearts, in the Lord's presence, "burned within them" impelling them to "tell their story" (cf. Lk 24:32; 35).

Today, the impediments to the spread of Christ's Kingdom are experienced most dramatically in the split between the Gospel and culture, with the exclusion of God from the public sphere. Canada has a well-earned reputation for a generous and practical commitment to justice and peace, and there is an enticing sense of vibrancy and opportunity in your multicultural cities. At the same time, however, certain values detached from their moral roots and full significance found in Christ have evolved in the most disturbing of ways. In the name of "tolerance" your country has had to endure the folly of the redefinition of spouse, and in the name of "freedom of choice" it is confronted with the daily destruction of unborn children. When the Creator's divine plan is ignored the truth of human nature is lost.

False dichotomies are not unknown within the Christian community itself. They are particularly damaging when Christian civic leaders sacrifice the unity of faith and sanction the disintegration of reason and the principles of natural ethics, by yielding to ephemeral social trends and the spurious demands of opinion polls. Democracy succeeds only to the extent that it is based on truth and a correct understanding of the human person. Catholic involvement in political life cannot compromise on this principle; otherwise Christian witness to the splendor of truth in the public sphere would be silenced and an autonomy from morality proclaimed (cf. Doctrinal Note *The Participation of Catholics in Political Life*, nos. 2-3; 6). In your discussions with politicians and civic leaders I encourage you to demonstrate that our Christian faith, far from being an impediment to dialogue, is a bridge, precisely because it brings together reason and culture.

4. Within the context of the evangelization of culture, I wish to mention the fine network of Catholic schools at the heart of ecclesial life in your Province. Catechesis and religious education is a taxing apostolate. I thank and encourage those many lay men and women, together with Religious, who strive to ensure that your young people become daily more appreciative of the gift of faith which they have received. More than ever this demands

that witness, nourished by prayer, be the all-encompassing milieu of every Catholic school. Teachers, as witnesses, account for the hope that nourishes their own lives (cf. 1 Pt 3:15) by living the truth they propose to their pupils, always in reference to the one they have encountered and whose dependable goodness they have sampled with joy (cf. Address to Rome's Ecclesial Diocesan Convention, *Living the Truth That God Loves His People*, June 6, 2005). And so with St. Augustine they say: "We who speak and you who listen acknowledge ourselves as fellow disciples of a single teacher" (St. Augustine, *Sermons*, 23:2).

A particularly insidious obstacle to education today, which your own reports attest, is the marked presence in society of that relativism which, recognizing nothing as definitive, leaves as the ultimate criterion only the self with its desires. Within such a relativistic horizon an eclipse of the sublime goals of life occurs with a lowering of the standards of excellence, a timidity before the category of the good, and a relentless but senseless pursuit of novelty parading as the realization of freedom. Such detrimental trends point to the particular urgency of the apostolate of "intellectual charity" which upholds the essential unity of knowledge, guides the young towards the sublime satisfaction of exercising their freedom in relation to truth, and articulates the relationship between faith and all aspects of family and civic life. Introduced to a love of truth, I am confident that young Canadians will relish exploring the house of the Lord who "enlightens every person who comes into the world" (Jn 1:9) and satisfies every desire of humanity.

5. Dear Brothers, with affection and fraternal gratitude I offer these reflections to you and encourage you in your proclamation of the Good News of Jesus Christ. Experience his love and in this way cause the light of God to enter into the world! (cf. *Deus Caritas Est*, no. 39). Invoking upon you the intercession of Mary, Seat of Wisdom, I cordially impart my Apostolic Blessing to you and the priests, Religious, and lay faithful of your dioceses.

BENEDICT XVI

Homily at Midnight Mass
St. Peter's Basilica
Sunday, December 24, 2006

God's Sign Is the Baby

Dear Brothers and Sisters,

We have just heard in the Gospel the message given by the angels to the shepherds during that Holy Night, a message which the Church now proclaims to us: "To you is born this day in the city of David a Savior, who is Christ the Lord. And this will be a sign for you: you will find a babe wrapped in swaddling clothes and lying in a manger" (Lk 2:11-12). Nothing miraculous, nothing extraordinary, nothing magnificent is given to the shepherds as a sign. All they will see is a child wrapped in swaddling clothes, one who, like all children, needs a mother's care; a child born in a stable, who therefore lies not in a cradle but in a manger. God's sign is the baby in need of help and in poverty. Only in their hearts will the shepherds be able to see that this baby fulfills the promise of the prophet Isaiah, which we heard in the first reading: "For to us a child is born, to us a son is given; and the government will be upon his shoulder" (Is 9:5). Exactly the same sign has been given to us. We too are invited by the angel of God, through the message of the Gospel, to set out in our hearts to see the child lying in the manger.

God's sign is simplicity. God's sign is the baby. God's sign is that he makes himself small for us. This is how he reigns. He does not come with power and outward splendor. He comes as a baby—defenseless and in need of our help. He does not want to overwhelm us with his strength. He takes away our fear of his greatness. He asks for our love: so he makes himself a child. He wants nothing other from us than our love, through which we spontaneously learn to enter into his feelings, his thoughts and his will—we learn to live with him and to practice with him that humility of renunciation that belongs to the very essence of love. God made himself small so that we could understand him, welcome him, and love him. The Fathers of the Church, in their Greek translation of the Old Testament, found a passage from the prophet Isaiah that Paul also quotes in order to show how God's new ways had already been foretold in the Old Testament. There we read: "God made his Word short, he abbreviated it" (Is 10:23; Rom 9:28). The Fathers interpreted this in two ways. The Son himself is the Word, the *Logos*; the eternal Word became small—small enough to fit into a manger. He became a child, so that the Word could be grasped by us. In this way God teaches us to love the little ones. In this way he teaches us to love the weak. In this way he teaches us respect for children. The child of Bethlehem directs our gaze toward all children who suffer and are abused in the world, the born and the unborn. Toward children who are placed as soldiers in a violent world; toward children who have to beg; toward children who suffer deprivation and hunger;

toward children who are unloved. In all of these it is the Child of Bethlehem who is crying out to us; it is the God who has become small who appeals to us. Let us pray this night that the brightness of God's love may enfold all these children. Let us ask God to help us do our part so that the dignity of children may be respected. May they all experience the light of love, which mankind needs so much more than the material necessities of life.

And so we come to the second meaning that the Fathers saw in the phrase: "God made his Word short." The Word which God speaks to us in Sacred Scripture had become long in the course of the centuries. It became long and complex, not just for the simple and unlettered, but even more so for those versed in Sacred Scripture, for the experts who evidently became entangled in details and in particular problems, almost to the extent of losing an overall perspective. Jesus "abbreviated" the Word—he showed us once more its deeper simplicity and unity. Everything taught by the Law and the Prophets is summed up—he says—in the command: "You shall love the Lord your God with all your heart, and with all your soul, and with all your mind . . . You shall love your neighbor as yourself" (Mt 22:37-40). This is everything—the whole faith is contained in this one act of love which embraces God and humanity. Yet now further questions arise: how are we to love God with all our mind, when our intellect can barely reach him? How are we to love him with all our heart and soul, when our heart can only catch a glimpse of him from afar, when there are so many contradictions in the world that would hide his face from us? This is where the two ways in which God has "abbreviated" his Word come together. He is no longer distant. He is no longer unknown. He is no longer beyond the reach of our heart. He has become a child for us, and in so doing he has dispelled all doubt. He has become our neighbor, restoring in this way the image of man, whom we often find so hard to love. For us, God has become a gift. He has given himself. He has entered time for us. He who is the Eternal One, above time, he has assumed our time and raised it to himself on high. Christmas has become the Feast of gifts in imitation of God who has given himself to us. Let us allow our heart, our soul and our mind to be touched by this fact! Among the many gifts that we buy and receive, let us not forget the true gift: to give each other something of ourselves, to give each other something of our time, to open our time to God. In this way anxiety disappears, joy is born, and the feast is created. During the festive meals of these days let us remember the Lord's words: "When you give a dinner or a banquet, do not invite those who will invite you in return, but invite those whom no one invites and who are not able to invite you" (cf. Lk 14:12-14). This also means: when you give gifts for Christmas, do not give only to those who will give to you in return, but give to those who receive from no one and who cannot give you anything back. This is what God has done: he invites us to his wedding feast, something which we cannot reciprocate, but can only receive with joy. Let us imitate him! Let us love God and, starting from him, let us also love man, so that, starting from man, we can then rediscover God in a new way!

And so, finally, we find yet a third meaning in the saying that the Word became "brief" and "small." The shepherds were told that they would find the child in a manger for animals, who were the rightful occupants of the stable. Reading Isaiah (1:3), the Fathers concluded that beside the manger of Bethlehem there stood an ox and an ass. At the same time they interpreted the text as symbolizing the Jews and the pagans—and thus all humanity—who each in their own way have need of a Savior: the God who became a child. Man, in order to live, needs bread, the fruit of the earth and of his labor. But he does not live by bread alone. He needs nourishment for his soul: he needs meaning that can fill his life. Thus, for the Fathers, the manger of the animals became the symbol of the altar, on which lies the Bread which is Christ himself: the true food for our hearts. Once again we see how he became small: in the humble appearance of the host, in a small piece of bread, he gives us himself.

All this is conveyed by the sign that was given to the shepherds and is given also to us: the child born for us, the child in whom God became small for us. Let us ask the Lord to grant us the grace of looking upon the crib this night with the simplicity of the shepherds, so as to receive the joy with which they returned home (cf. Lk 2:20). Let us ask him to give us the humility and the faith with which St. Joseph looked upon the child that Mary had conceived by the Holy Spirit. Let us ask the Lord to let us look upon him with that same love with which Mary saw him. And let us pray that in this way the light that the shepherds saw will shine upon us too, and that what the angels sang that night will be accomplished throughout the world: "Glory to God in the highest, and on earth peace among men with whom he is pleased." Amen!

Chronology of the Life of Jesus

6-4 BC (7-6)[1]

Jesus is born in Bethlehem of Judea (Mt 2:1, 5, 6; Lk 2:4-7), under the reign of Herod the Great (Mt 2:1; Lk 1:5) and the empire of Caesar Augustus (Lk 2:1). Bethlehem was the home town of Jesus' parents, where—according to Luke's account—they had returned from their home in Nazareth in order to register in a census commanded by the emperor Augustus, when the governor of the Roman province of Syria was Publius Sulpicius Quirinius (Lk 2:2; Acts 5:37), between AD 6 and 7.

In Bethlehem, then, the city of David, Mary—engaged to Joseph, but pregnant by the work of the Holy Spirit— gives birth, in a "manger" (Lk 2:7, 12, 16), to the Messiah proclaimed by the prophets, who is given the name Jesus (Mt 1:18-25). His birth, however, rather than being referred to the years of the Quirinian census, seems rather to be situated a few years before the death of Herod (Mt 2:15-19), which took place between March 12 and April 11 of 4 BC.

---

1   Because it is impossible to establish exact dates, the more probable hypotheses are highlighted in bold, without omitting other well-founded hypotheses (indicated in parentheses).

As for the day of Jesus' birth, this is fixed by ancient Christian tradition at December 25, unlike other traditions that set it at other dates (January 6 or 10, November 18, March 28). The choice of December 25 is connected to the fact that this day, in conjunction with the winter solstice (the triumph of the sun over the darkness), is particularly suited to celebrating the birth of Christ, "sun of justice" (Mal 3:20). The feast of Christmas first emerged in Rome around the year 336, although it is mentioned for the first time in 354.

The salient episodes that accompany the birth of Jesus in the Gospel accounts are: the circumcision on the eighth day (Lk 2:21) and his presentation at the temple of Jerusalem; the purification ritual and consecration to the Lord (Lk 2:22-24); the visit of the shepherds to the manger (Lk 2:8-20); the coming of the Magi from the East (Mt 2:1-12) and the flight to Egypt of Joseph, with Mary and the child, in order to escape from Herod (Mt 2:13-23).

There is no information about the childhood and adolescence of Jesus. But it can be supposed, from elements of fact and from various indications, that in his family of craftsmen, modest but with sufficient means, Jesus received a basic education, learned a trade, and from the religious point of view, was raised as a normal Jewish boy, trained to listen to and read the Scriptures, to frequent the synagogue, and to observe the laws and devotional practices.

AD 4-6 (6-8)

At the age of twelve (Lk 2:42), Jesus encounters the teachers in the temple (Lk 2:41-50).

28-29 (25-26)

The beginning of the ministry of Jesus, at around the age of thirty (Lk 3:23)—a number that, as for Joseph (Gn 41:46) and David (2 Sm 5:4), is intended above all to indicate the age of full human maturity—must be connected with the beginning of the preaching of John the Baptist, in the fifteenth year (Lk 3:1-2) of the empire of Tiberius Caesar (28-29), the successor of Augustus. This span of time includes the Baptism of Jesus in the Jordan (Mt 3:13-17; Mk 1:9-11; Lk 3:21-22; Jn 1:29-34) administered by John, who lived as an ascetic in the desert of Judea and, proclaiming the imminence of the Kingdom of God, urged repentance and the purification of sins through the Baptism of conversion.

Immediately after his Baptism, Jesus goes into the desert, where he is tempted by Satan (Mt 4:1-11; Mk 1:12-13; Lk 4:1-13), who wants above all to ruin Jesus' relationship of love and fidelity with the Father and instead ends up reinforcing his awareness of being the Son of God who must carry out the great mission for which he has been sent into the world.

After spending forty days in the desert, Jesus, accompanied by the three disciples who were the first to follow him (Andrew, John, and Simon Peter), goes into the low country of Galilee (the territory of Herod Antipas), preaching and healing. During a wedding feast in Cana, he performs his first miracle, turning water into wine (Jn 2:1-11).

From Cana he goes to Capernaum, which would remain the center of his activity in Galilee, and from there to Jerusalem, to celebrate the Jewish Passover (Jn 2:13). Here, on the occasion of the first of the three Passovers cited by John (Jn 2:13, 23; 6:4; 11:55)—unlike the synoptics that mention only one of them (Mt 26:17; Mk 14:1; Lk 22:1)—Jesus drives the moneychangers out of the temple (Jn 2:15-16). In Jerusalem the nighttime encounter with Nicodemus also takes place (Jn 3:1-21).

After leaving Jerusalem, Jesus goes to an unspecified location in Judea (Jn 3:22) along the Jordan River, east of Jericho, where his disciples baptize (Jn 4:2). Then he goes through Samaria to Galilee (Jn 4:3-4) and, during this voyage, the encounter with the Samaritan woman takes place in Sychar, at the well of Jacob (Jn 4:5-7). Having arrived in Galilee, he receives in Cana an official of the king, who implores and obtains the healing of his son (Jn 4:46-54). He gets back on the road to Jerusalem to attend "a feast of the Jews" (Jn 5:1): this may have been Pentecost or the feast of Booths, but not Passover. Near the pool called Bethesda, located near the Sheep Gate (Jn 5:2), Jesus heals the paralytic (Jn 5:8-9).

Immediately after the arrest of John the Baptist (Mt 14:3; Mk 1:14; Lk 3:20)—decapitated in the same year, AD 29 (Mt 14:1-12; Mk 6:14-29; Lk 9:7-9)—Jesus begins to preach in Galilee; he visits the synagogue of Nazareth and there, commenting on the passage of Isaiah 61:1-2, he illustrates his universal mission of salvation; in Capernaum he teaches, heals the sick, drives out demons, performs miracles (Mk 1:16-20, 21-34; Lk 4:31-37; 5:1-11). From Capernaum to Bethesda to Caesarea Philippi: it is a whole series of events, discourses, and miracles that see Jesus as their protagonist.

30

Then begins the voyage toward Jerusalem, through Perea. Arriving in Bethany, he resuscitates his friend Lazarus (Jn 11:38-45); from there he heads toward Jericho, where he heals the blind beggar Bartimaeus (Mk 10:46-52; Lk 18:35-43) and converts the rich tax collector Zacchaeus (Lk 19:1-10).

The last week of Jesus' life—six days before Passover—can be summed up as follows. Between Saturday evening and Sunday Jesus arrives in Bethany (Jn 12:1); on Sunday, he encounters the crowd. On Monday, he makes his triumphant entry into Jerusalem (Mt 21:1-11; Mk 11:1-11; Lk 19:28-38); on Tuesday, he curses the sterile fig tree (Mt 21:18-19; Mk 11:12-14) and drives the money-changers out of the temple (Mt 21:12-13; Mk 11:15-17; Lk 19:45-46); on Wednesday, he faces the dispute in the temple (Mt 21:23-27, 39; Mk 11:27-12:44; Lk 20:1-21:4) and proclaims the destruction of Jerusalem and the persecutions of the disciples (Mt 24:1–25:46; Mk 13:1-37; Lk 21:5-36); on Thursday, he sits at table with the Twelve (Mt 26:20-30; Mk 14:17-26; Lk 22:14-30); he is arrested (Mt 26:47-56; Mk 14:43-52; Lk 22:47-53; Jn 18:2-12) and led before the high priest Caiaphas (Mt 26:57-75; Mk 14:53-72; Lk 22:54-65; Jn 18:13-27); on Friday, he is led before the Sanhedrin (Mt 27:1; Mk 15:1; Lk 22:66); he is then handed over to the fifth governor of Judea (26-37), Pontius Pilate (Mt 27:2-30; Mk 15:2-19; Lk 23:1-25; Jn 18:28–19:16); finally, he is crucified and buried (Mt 27:31-60; Mk

15:20-46; Lk 23:26-54; Jn 19:16-42). On Saturday, he lies in the tomb; on Sunday, he rises (Mt 28:1-15; Mk 16:1-8; 24:1-35).

In this context, the Last Supper of Thursday evening—during which Jesus gives his disciples their last important instructions before he leaves them—opens a decisive phase, both from the perspective of the succession of events and as a symbolic act on the part of Jesus to affirm the meaning and the expiatory efficacy of his death. From the place of the supper, Jesus goes to the garden of Gethsemane, where he stops and spends a long time in prayer. Here Judas, the traitor, delivers him up to the guards sent by the high priests to arrest him (Mk 14:43-52). Led before Annas and then before Caiaphas, Jesus is subjected, throughout the night and the early morning, to a series of interrogations that constitute the so-called "trial" of Jesus.

Before the complete assembly of the Sanhedrin, Jesus is at first accused of having threatened to destroy the temple and then found guilty of having blasphemed against God (Mt 26:59-68; Mk 14:58-63; Lk 22:67-71). On the basis of this formal sentence, the penalty stipulated by Jewish law was death, the execution of which was the responsibility of the Roman prefect. Since for Roman law the accusation of blasphemy was not sufficient for such a penalty, Jesus is brought before Pontius Pilate, with the accusation of having incited the people to rebellion and of having claimed the title of "king of the Jews." Pilate realizes that the accusations against Jesus as a political revolutionary are a pretense, and, already an adversary of the Jews, he tries to outmaneuver the system to foil the death penalty against

Jesus: according to Luke 23:6-12, even by transferring the case to the jurisdiction of Herod, since Jesus came from Galilee. In any case, Pilate—convinced of Jesus' innocence (Lk 23:2-22)—tries to set him free, using the traditional Passover amnesty (Mk 15:6-15) and, seeing the attempt fail because of the stubborn hostility toward Jesus on the part of the crowd—so instigated as to be willing to free a bandit like Barabbas, just to see Jesus condemned to death—tries to resolve the case by subjecting Jesus to flagellation (Jn 19:1), with the idea that this would be enough to spare him from capital punishment. But the threatening insistence of the Jewish leaders (Jn 19:12)—who had evidently already decided to execute Jesus—puts Pilate up against the ropes. Jesus is condemned to crucifixion.

Burdened with the Cross, Jesus walks the way of Calvary, helped in the last stage of the journey by a Cyrenean. At Golgotha—the "place of the skull" (Mt 27:33; Mk 15:22; Lk 23:33; Jn 19:17)—he is crucified, and, despite undergoing derision and outrages, speaks only words of forgiveness and intercession before dying. This attitude does not fail to stir up strong emotions among the bystanders, even in the Roman centurion (Mk 15:39) and in the "good thief" who is crucified next to him (Lk 23:40-42). Dying, Jesus entrusts himself to the Father (Lk 23:46), sealing his life and mission with the words, "It is finished" (Jn 19:30). He is buried in a tomb dug into the rock, which, on Sunday morning, is found empty by the women who have run to the tomb.

Jesus rises from the dead, and with his Resurrection comes the central and decisive event of faith, of apostolic experience, and of Christian preaching. On the road to Emmaus, Jesus appears to two disciples (Lk 24:13-35) and later to the apostles (Lk 24:36-43), to whom he gives the last instructions about their future ministry (Lk 24:44-48) before ascending into heaven (Lk 24:50-53).

Writings on the Gospels and the History of Jesus

Karl Adam, *Gesù il Cristo*. Trans. Pietro De Ambroggi, Brescia: Morcelliana, 1995.

Jean-Noël Aletti, *Jésus-Christ fait-il l'unité du Nouveau Testament?* Éditions Desclée, 1994.

Angelo Amato, *Gesù il Signore. Saggio di cristologia*. Bologna: EDB, 2003.

Giuseppe Barbaglio, *Gesù ebreo di Galilea. Indagine storica*. Bologna: EDB, 2002.

Klaus Berger, *Jesus*. Munich: Pattloch Verlag, 2004.

Marcello Bordoni, *Gesù di Nazaret, Signore e Cristo: Saggio di cristologia sistematica*. Rome: Herder, 1982-1986, 3 vols.

Marcello Bordoni, *Gesù di Nazaret: Presenza, memoria, attesa*. Brescia: Queriniana, 2004.

Marcello Bordoni, *Christus omnium redemptor. Saggi di cristologia*. Vatican City: Libreria Editrice Vaticana, 2010.

Franco Giulio Brambilla, *Il Crocifisso risorto. Risurrezione di Gesù e fede dei discepoli*. Brescia: Queriniana, 1999.

Raymond E. Brown, *The Death of the Messiah: From Gethsemane to the Grave*. New York: The Anchor Bible Reference Library, Doubleday, 1994.

Raymond E. Brown, *The Birth of the Messiah: A Commentary on the Infancy Narratives in the Gospels of Matthew and Luke*. New York: The Anchor Bible Reference Library, Doubleday, 1999.

Adriana Destro and Mauro Pesce, *Encounters with Jesus: The Man in His Place and Time*. Minneapolis: Fortress Press, 2012.

James D.G. Dunn, *Jesus Remembered: Christianity in the Making*. Grand Rapids, MI: William B. Eerdmans Publishing Company, 2003.

Rinaldo Fabris, *Gesù di Nazareth. Storia e interpretazione*. Assisi, Cittadella, 1999.

Rino Fisichella, *Gesù di Nazaret: Profezia del Padre*, Milano: Paoline, 2000.

Bruno Forte, *Gesù di Nazaret: Storia di Dio, Dio della storia*. Cinisello Balsamo: Edizioni San Paolo, 2007.

Sean Freyne, *Jesus, a Jewish Galilean: A New Reading of the Jesus Story*. New York: T&T Clark International, 2004.

Joachim Gnilka, *Jesus of Nazareth: Message and History.* Trans. Siegfried S. Schatzmann. Peabody, MA: Hendrickson Publishers, Inc., 1997.

Maurizio Gronchi and Juvénal Llunga Muja, *Gesù di Nazaret: Un personaggio storico.* Milan: Paoline, 2005.

Romano Guardini, *The Lord.* Trans. Elinor Castendyk Briefs. Washington, DC: Regnery Publishing, Inc., 1982.

Larry W. Hurtado, *Lord Jesus Christ: Devotion to Jesus in Earliest Christianity.* Grand Rapids, MI: Wm. B. Eerdmans Publishing Co., 2003.

Walter Kasper, *The God of Jesus Christ.* New York: T&T Clark International, 2012.

Walter Kasper, *Jesus the Christ.* Trans. V. Green. Mahwah, NJ: Paulist Press, 1977.

Hans Kessler, *Sucht den Lebenden nicht bei den Toten: Die Auferstehung Jesu Christi in biblischer, fundamentaltheologischer und systematischer Sicht.* Düsseldorf: Patmos, 1985.

Xavier Léon-Dufour, *The Gospels and the Jesus of History.* New York: Doubleday, 1967.

Franco Manzi, *Memoria del Risorto e testimonianza della Chiesa*, Assisi: Cittadella, 2006.

John P. Meier, *A Marginal Jew: Rethinking the Historical Jesus*. New York: The Anchor Yale Bible Reference Library, 1991-2009, 4 vols.

Romano Penna, *I ritratti originali di Gesù il Cristo: Inizi e sviluppi della cristologia neotestamentaria*. Cinisello Balsamo, Edizioni San Paolo, 1996-1999, 2 vols.

Charles Perrot, *Jésus, Christ et Seigneur des premiers Chrétiens: Une christologie exegetique*. Editions Desclée, 1997.

Armand Puig i Tàrrech, *Gesù: La risposta agli enigmi*, Trans. Samantha Zanati. Cinisello Balsamo, Edizioni San Paolo, 2007.

Joseph Ratzinger (Pope Benedict XVI), *Jesus of Nazareth*. San Francisco: Ignatius Press, 2007, 2 vols.

Rudolf Schnackenburg, *La persona di Gesù nei quattro vangeli*. Trans. Franco Bassani, Brescia: Paideia, 1995.

Jacques Schlosser, *Jésus de Nazareth*. Paris: Éditions Noesis, 1999.

Heinz Schürmann, *Jesu ureigener Tod: Exegetische Besinnungen und Ausblick*. Freiburg: Herder, 1976.

Albert Schweitzer, *The Quest of the Historical Jesus: A Critical Study of Its Progress from Reimarus to Wrede*. Trans. W. Montgomery. Macmillan, 1954.

Giuseppe Segalla, *Sulle tracce di Gesù: La "terza ricerca."* Assisi: Cittadella, 2006.

Bernard Sesboüé, *Jésus-Christ: L'unique médiateur.* Editions Desclée, 1988.

Gerd Theissen and Annette Merz, *The Historical Jesus; A Comprehensive Guide.* Minneapolis: Fortress Press, 1998.

Geza Vermes, *Jesus the Jew: A Historian's Reading of the Gospels.* Philadelphia: Fortress Press, 1981.